GW00400253

Self-Coaching Leadership

Further praise for Self-Coaching Leadership

'. . . so many new models and processes to use it felt like Christmas – they are great and so effective . . .'

Karen Donley, HR Director, MBDA, BAe

'. . . provides a rich resource for all those concerned with raising the bar on senior management and leadership performance, whether as the executive in question or his/her coach or advisor.'

David Hoad, Director, The Kingsmoor Consultancy

'A practical workshop manual to have open as you tackle the challenges of life as a manager. Do the exercises and make this book work for you – you will find it is like an experienced coach; it gives you the tools to do a better job, relax, learn and grow at the same time.'

Tim Nottidge, General Manager, Business Development, BT Global Services

'It provides an excellent introduction to being able to consider "how" executives can improve their self management and the management of others within the limited time available, while facing ever increasing pressures. It also set out a more detailed methodology to follow to take practical steps which will help to achieve the benefits which we all seek.'

DC, HR Director, multi-billion turn-over NGO

'Beautifully congruent. This book doesn't dictate what you should do to be a leader – it provides examples, models and inspiration so you acquire exquisite leadership skills in the reading of it.'

James Lawley and Penny Tompkins, authors of *Metaphors in Mind: Transformation through Symbolic Modelling*

'I would recommend this book to any manager or leader who really wants to get ahead.'

Veronica Lim, Executive Coach, www.veronicalim.com

'The book is the perfect blend of well resourced information grounded with relevant examples and exercises that allow the reader to work through the whole book or to build on a particular skill and would be a useful addition to your bookshelf.'

Camilla Arnold, Director of Talent, TXG Ltd

Self-Coaching Leadership

Simple Steps from Manager to Leader

Angus I. McLeod, PhD

JOSSEY-BASS
A Wiley Imprint
www.josseybass.com

Copyright © 2007   John Wiley & Sons Ltd, The Atrium, Southern Gate, Chichester,
West Sussex PO19 8SQ, England

Telephone   (+44) 1243 779777

Under the Jossey-Bass imprint, Jossey-Bass, 989 Market Street, San Francisco CA 94103-1741,
USA
www.jossey-bass.com

Email (for orders and customer service enquiries): cs-books@wiley.co.uk
Visit our Home Page on www.wiley.com

All Rights Reserved. No part of this publication may be reproduced, stored in a retrieval
system or transmitted in any form or by any means, electronic, mechanical, photocopying,
recording, scanning or otherwise, except under the terms of the Copyright, Designs and
Patents Act 1988 or under the terms of a licence issued by the Copyright Licensing Agency
Ltd, 90 Tottenham Court Road, London W1T 4LP, UK, without the permission in writing of
the Publisher. Requests to the Publisher should be addressed to the Permissions Department,
John Wiley & Sons Ltd, The Atrium, Southern Gate, Chichester, West Sussex PO19 8SQ,
England, or emailed to permreq@wiley.co.uk, or faxed to (+44) 1243 770620.

Designations used by companies to distinguish their products are often claimed as trademarks.
All brand names and product names used in this book are trade names, service marks,
trademarks or registered trademarks of their respective owners. The Publisher is not
associated with any product or vendor mentioned in this book.

This publication is designed to provide accurate and authoritative information in regard to the
subject matter covered. It is sold on the understanding that the Publisher is not engaged in
rendering professional services. If professional advice or other expert assistance is required,
the services of a competent professional should be sought.

Other Wiley Editorial Offices

John Wiley & Sons Inc., 111 River Street, Hoboken, NJ 07030, USA

Jossey-Bass, 989 Market Street, San Francisco, CA 94103-1741, USA

Wiley-VCH Verlag GmbH, Boschstr. 12, D-69469 Weinheim, Germany

John Wiley & Sons Australia Ltd, 42 McDougall Street, Milton, Queensland 4064, Australia

John Wiley & Sons (Asia) Pte Ltd, 2 Clementi Loop #02-01, Jin Xing Distripark, Singapore
129809

John Wiley & Sons Canada Ltd, 6045 Freemont Blvd, Mississauga, ONT, L5R 4J3, Canada

Wiley also publishes its books in a variety of electronic formats. Some content that appears in
print may not be available in electronic books.

Anniversary Logo Design: Richard J. Pacifico

British Library Cataloguing in Publication Data

A catalogue record for this book is available from the British Library

ISBN 978-0-470-51280-7 (HB)

Typeset in 11/16pt Trump Medieval by SNP Best-set Typesetter Ltd., Hong Kong
Printed and bound in Great Britain by TJ International Ltd, Padstow, Cornwall, UK
This book is printed on acid-free paper responsibly manufactured from sustainable forestry in
which at least two trees are planted for each one used for paper production.

To Dr Gordon Signy

Contents

List of illustrations

About the author

ANGUS MCLEOD WAS AN ACADEMIC RESEARCH scientist before moving into industry, where he held a number of roles, first in technical management including quality, then in marketing and sales. He moved into general management including COO and Chairmanship jobs before moving into consultancy. He has held numerous commercial directorships and continues to sit on a number of company boards, mostly in the environmental and training and development sectors. His business experience includes a buy-in MBO for an international financial institution. His consultancy experience in the last 10 years has developed into leadership, team development as well as executive and performance coaching. He and his colleagues offer facilitation, course design, training in a multitude of management and leadership skills as well as providing coaching, mentoring and supporting consultancy.

Dr McLeod is widely published in leading journals in the USA and the UK where his business is primarily directed. He wrote

Me, Myself, My Team (Crown House, 2000; 2nd edition, 2006) which focuses on the development of personal qualities of all those who work in teams and the application of that learning for team development. He wrote the widely-acclaimed book *Performance Coaching: The Handbook for Managers, HR Professionals and Coaches* (Crown House, 2003), which is the practical resource book featuring real coaching situations and dialogues. He designed the 13-day Diploma-Course in Performance Coaching for Newcastle College with over 7,000 student registrations in its first year (2004) and assisted in the development of standards in coaching and mentoring for the UK (2005). He travels widely and regularly contributes at conferences around the world.

Dr McLeod co-founded the Coaching Foundation Ltd in the late 1990s. This is a not-for-profit organization helping to develop best practice in both executive and life-coaching and exposing the membership to a wide range of new thinking. He also runs personal development courses including the *Question of Balance, Wellbeing from Healthy Thinking* and the *Write-One* writing course in a number of countries.

He was the motivator for *Ask Max*, the internet-based e-mentoring service which is available via his organization, Angus McLeod Associates.

Dr McLeod has bachelor and doctoral degrees in science. He is trained in NLP and co-counseling and has a Diploma in Performance Coaching. Dr McLeod is also a Master Meta-Coach and a member of the International Society of Neuro-Semantics. He is a full member of the Neuro-linguistic Psychotherapy Counseling Association.

He is a keen motorcyclist, involved in training to advanced levels. He is also a competitive rower and Chairman of his club. He works from Philadelphia in the USA and from the West Midlands in the UK.

www.angusmcleod.com

contact:

ourinfo@angusmcleod.com

Preface

TONY IS THE OPERATIONS DIRECTOR FOR A MAJOR international, manufacturing business. It's a job he has had just over 12 months after being recruited to 'move and shake'. As a result of his efforts, throughput has doubled. He works long and hard, thinks carefully about strategic change and gets the job done. The urgent period of change is now almost complete and he needs his people to be more independent – making solutions and suggesting more ideas to improve productivity. Tony is bright and knows that he needs to start changing his management style if he is to continue in the present role. The time for telling people what to do and how to do it must end, and there needs to be a period when people are more involved in the solutions by taking more initiative and responsibility. Tony also needs greater involvement from his people to enable him to spend less time in the day-to-day operations, and more time on the bigger structures and strategies that lie ahead. However, in meetings he notices that when he asks a question, he rarely gets a response. His people are used to Tony giving them directions.

Tony has read a great deal about managing and has implemented many current ideas to help his people to take risks and use their initiative. However, they are still highly dependent upon him, so what should he do now?

This book is for people like Tony and the many people I coach, some of whom are at the top of their profession. It is not a handbook of leadership but a collection of learnings based upon the real experiences and enormous changes that these people have made in the last couple of years in particular. It provides 'can-do' strategies for change that you can implement immediately. The people I coach, by and large, are already high earners, heading up large teams and responsible for very large financials. Through their own learning in a few sessions, they mainly report that they are more effective, work fewer hours, are more strategic, have better and more motivated people and work in a noticeably different way – so much different that a number are unexpectedly promoted within a few months of the end of the coaching assignment. The learning from which these people benefited is contained in this book and may help to put you on a similar fast-track to promotion, or a new job.

Generally, leadership is about influence, encouraging our people to follow us. Managing tends to be a process of pushing people somewhere. The ideas and solutions in this book deal with both of these administerial approaches. We continuously need to manage as well as lead, and I offer a model that defines managing and leading and lets you know the approach that can be most effectively used, and when. I present tools and strategies to assist you in developing your own unique ways of managing and leading.

Self-challenge and greater self-awareness are at the heart of our development as leaders. These two characteristics offer us more choices in the way we choose to work and help us to understand others better – to motivate them more effectively – and Part Three of this text is largely concerned with development at this level.

The 'Real Thing', the genuine nature of self, is often sidelined – many of us tend to manage using an adopted style; something borrowed, something new, evolving over time. But modern leadership demands a more flexible approach. People, their aspirations and their demands have changed. We need to adapt to keep the edge. One of those edges is the elegant use of the 'Real Thing', or authenticity. And the Real Thing is invariably more impactful than acting a part. So Part Three also develops ideas to help develop and use your authenticity intelligently; to impact and inspire others to follow you.

As far as possible, as with my training work, I illustrate real-life applications to enable you to decide what may be useful to you and how you might adapt the ideas to address your own challenges. If you take just one thing and apply it successfully, then I am content. To assist in that, this book is heavily indexed.

The book is organized into three main sections: Part One looks specifically at leadership of self and offers practical methods for change, impact and efficiency at the next level. Many of these methods have been tested and applied by managers and leaders who have made that transformation.

Part Two begins to apply much of that learning in leading those around us. It is unapologetically directed at those methods that influence the people we connect with – a practical set of methodologies rather than a textbook of strategic management for organizational change. It directs attention at applied leadership as it influences people to perform for you. A great deal of the content springs from real ideas, methods and strategies that are applied by highly successful people whom I have coached or who have been delegates of mine. I have emphasized ideas that can be applied immediately at work – often to all stakeholders in the organization, and not just those who work for us directly. Objectives include being able to make better decisions, to increase motivation in teams and to create more sustainable organizations.

Part Three extends the practical aspects of personal leadership with a greater level of stretch. The purpose is to develop a greater awareness of self as leader and to control and increase the number of development steps that will make a specific difference to you. The 'Real Thing' is also presented there.

It is worth noting that the significant items in Parts One and Two offer direct applications for encouraging those who work for us. If we can stimulate our people (and other stakeholders) to appreciate leader-thinking, then the whole of our team, and even the whole of the organizational culture, is going to shift to higher levels of efficacy.

The index is designed to help you to find your way about and to make the search for something previously seen as easy as possible.

Be inspirational; join the group of great and successful leaders,

Mt Airy,
Philadelphia, PA

Acknowledgments

MANY FRIENDS AROUND THE WORLD HELP BY BEING positive and unsurprised by my vision. They rarely wish me 'good luck' but instead express their confidence – leaders everywhere will recognize the difference in those two approaches. Friends forgive my disappearances and welcome me back. They know who they are and I love and appreciate every one of them. I hope that any gap between the extent of that love and their understanding of it is narrowed in reading these words.

Particular thanks are warmly due to Dr Adrienne Carpenter who created the writing space and made wholly illegible editing notes, much to my amusement. I am indebted to Captain Frank Biller of the celebrated Fairmount Club on Boathouse Row. He saved me from sinking into the author's pit by inviting me to sweep-oar with him and his members at any time.

Thanks to my business partner in Ireland, Michael Byrne, who provided advice on the first draft and the most wonderful hospitality in his beautiful country. Thanks also to David Dove and my colleagues at 3CCCs for their understanding at my absences.

I wish to thank the many successful coachees who have inspired me with their willingness to risk and achieve. You have provided me with the most enthralling part of my education in coaching and leadership – it was also the cheapest part!

Last, but not least, my thanks go to Lynne Stirling who offered advice at a time when her own management and leadership skills were needed elsewhere.

Part One
Leadership of Self

L EADERSHIP IS NOT SIMPLY DEFINED BY OUR ACTIONS AND the way we influence those around us. Leadership arises out of personal abilities that are beyond the average in many ways. Common characteristics include:

- Introspection

- Self-challenge

- Making personal stretch-goals of increasing size and impact

- Seeking out a wider range of solutions than those that arise from experience

- Listening well

- Being very clear

- Creating clear visions and goals.

For these reasons Part One is dedicated to the management, self-coaching and leadership of self. The content is designed to test and stretch, and to provide models for gaining new perspectives, widening personal choice and behaving differently and more successfully at work.

We might start with an issue facing the majority of top managers in organizations everywhere – Time.

1

Time

TODAY'S SENIOR EXECUTIVES MAINLY SHARE THE principal issues of a huge workload and a perceived lack of time. What is also true is that, through coaching, this invariably changes in a remarkable way without loss of impact, results or esteem. How is that possible?

John is Group HR Director of an internationally significant manufacturing business in the aviation sector. When I met with him it was clear that he was an effective individual with a great deal of knowledge and experience. He was the second highest paid director in the business, a consistently high performer. The cost side to this was the state of his health (hypertension) and his sense of wellbeing. John was working at least 50 percent more than his contracted commitment, traveling a great deal and trying to live in two different locations. Within a few hours of coaching over a month or so, he had made a significant number of changes. These included leaving work by 6 p.m. on most days when not traveling, taking up his preferred sports and hobbies again, arranging to set up an office near his home and work from there most Mondays and Fridays (thus having four days near home rather than one and a half), setting up a new home-from-home in his other location rather than living in a hotel, resigning from a number of operational meetings and seconding members of his team to other meetings where appropriate.

Kate was a comparatively young, Technology Development Director in a major electronics business and had numerous Project Heads reporting to her. Kate told me over a few hours of coaching that she had been running high-capex projects for a few years but it had been noted by her COO that her position at Board now required a more strategic and holistic application of her knowledge and experience. Also, Kate had leap-frogged over colleagues, and a number of very competent people now reported to Kate or to her direct reports. This was creating ongoing difficulties. Her private life was a mess and she was literally married to the business.

Within a few hours of coaching over two or three months, Kate had made enormous progress. Her Project Heads were brought together to develop strategic networking opportunities for co-work and relationship management with colleagues in other countries. At the next level down, technical people were seconded in and out of the organization to improve company-to-company relations and impact on best practice. Kate started to turn down corporate representative opportunities at the many hospitality functions available to senior members in the business and went back to her main sport. She stopped smoking and spent more time with her children.

She developed far-reaching strategic plans for the integration of technology across the businesses and was promoted within three months to the International Board.

These events are typical. We all know the key pressures on anyone's time, and the standard answers, and still we work 20, 30 or 40 hours a week more than we should. So what stops so many of us from changing that?

Lock-in syndrome

The 'lock-in syndrome' (LIS) is a patterned response to pressure of work (whether externally real or self-generated). As the demands go up, we stretch the day. We start traveling on Sunday evenings, work a few hours each evening when at home, arrive at the office an hour before anyone else to clear the desk and leave two hours later than most people to catch-up on outstanding actions (and needs from peers and immediate bosses).

Once the pattern has started, the intense focus on work and action means that the ability to focus more widely is lost. You are already locked-in. It takes a major catastrophe or critical personal event to stimulate the revaluing of what we do and why we do it. As leaders, it is necessary not to follow the pattern blindly but, on entering that pattern of our own choice and will, we must exercise choice, review the options and, if necessary, back out.

To counteract the effect of lock-in, we need to see a wider picture of what is happening. There are a number of things that, with awareness, might make a difference and enable us to take control of the situation:

- Recalibrate the relative importance of what we do in the greater context of our contributions in all our work.

- Prioritizing our health and wellbeing to ensure that we stay well and can contribute.

- Rethink the contribution we make to our families or friends.

- Realize that having trained our head to be busy, stillness demands effort of will to become rehabituated for creative thought.

- Break our workday habits – change the start of each working day as much as possible.

- Work out where our contributions are most essential, setting out areas of essential influence and delegating and withdrawing from unessential functions/demands. Delegate more.

- Think about the skills and competencies of our immediate people (and therefore who is really best able to take over key tasks and when) and the level of support to offer them.

These actions are designed to gain wider perspective and to be calmer and more effective. Breaking workday habits is something we will flesh out in more detail later. It is important because the lock-in syndrome (LIS) originates from patterned learning where we have lost full personal control.

Fire-fighting

Fire-fighting is the precursor to LIS (when the individual is no longer able to return to a relaxed state of being). Fire-fighting is not wrong per se if consciously chosen as a temporary need with a specific end, and if one can regain one's composure after that need has passed. The danger comes when the 'high' associated with one episode is so exciting[1] that the person is unable to calm down again. Instead, he or she compulsively goes to the next fire-fight, and if there isn't one, tends to make a drama in order to create one. Thus, LIS is a patterned behavior that arises when one starts to go from one fire-fight to the next without a pause for reflection, perspective and the deliberate use of choice. Since patterns often develop subconsciously, there are real dangers in being exposed to situations where multiple and sequential fire-fights are the norm. Repeated fire-fights may lead the person to LIS with no knowledge of how he or she arrived there!

Fire-fights are common in task-oriented businesses running to tight schedules and pressures. Many of us used to associate fire-fighting with lower and middle management, but these days fire-fighting has infected the highest levels in many organizations. Fire-fighting at this level creates incipient

---

[1] Highs are triggered by the release of adrenaline.

weakness. If most of our work is concerned with putting out fires, tactical decisions may be made but the strategic development of the business, in the myriad of areas in which this is essential for sustainability, must fall short. If fire-fighting characterizes the bulk of your work life, what can you do?

Earlier, I suggested changing the beginning of each day. This can start at home or at the hotel. The earlier in the day you make these changes, the better the impact of the result. Patterns are triggered by a sequence of psychological events that run rapidly and sequentially, and usually out of conscious awareness or control. To challenge the pattern, it is necessary to break it at an early part of the sequence. There are many things that can make a difference, including:

- Consider taking a morning walk for about 10 minutes, if you do not already do this. Buying a dog can save your life if it helps you to exercise and slow down. It can also save a relationship if you sometimes share this activity with a partner. If you have no aerobic exercises at present, consider including some in your morning routine.

- If you take stimulants, such as caffeine (in coffee, tea and chocolate), nicotine (smoking of tobacco), beta-carotene (in fizzy, especially yellow and orange drinks, pastilles and lozenges), then consider starting the day without them and replace them with other desired foods/activities.

- If you start the day by dealing with mail or email, schedule this activity for later in the morning. Mail requires a series of quick action loops – think–decision–action, think–decision–action – and these stimulate the mind into a fire-fighting pattern . . . tda, tda, tda (Figure 1.1). If you get hooked into that cycle, a whole day can be lost. You may have been active, but how productive have you been? And what contribution have you made to life tomorrow, next month, next year or 10 years ahead?

It is best to start each day with a period of reflection. Nobody told you that that was useful before they promoted you again and again! Thoughtful, strategic consideration will also get the mind to work in evolutionary processes rather than a rapid decision mode. With luck, your mind will be more able to return to this strategic work later, even if you are in fire-fighting in between. The mind is like a muscle: use it differently and often and it becomes more flexible, with quicker reactions.

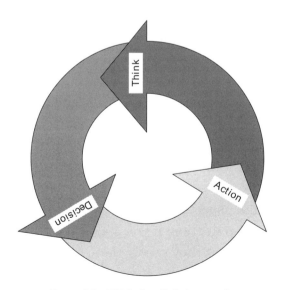

Figure 1.1   TDA fire-fighting cycle

The type of strategic thinking you could address may include:

1. Who else is influential in supporting or undermining my function and what can I do to create a better environment for the success of my function?

2. Which parts of my function could be managed elsewhere (in or outside the business) and are any of these options viable and useful to the business and, if so, what can I do to influence that change or protect that area from a less-effective option?

3. Of the major things that need to be communicated in the next period, when would be the best time to communicate them, who should be involved in advance of that, and how should the communication strategy be planned and carried out?

4. Who misunderstands me, the way I work or my motives, and what might I do to get them on-side?

5. What are the strengths, weaknesses and perceived potential of my immediate reports and what can be done to test their perceived potential and assist them in taking on more responsibility?

These are large aspect questions that demand a period of thought and self-reflection. If you are creating your own questions, make sure that they satisfy these criteria. The demands should not be urgent as this may encourage stress responses and periods of rapid judgment without thinking-through solutions in significant depth. Urgency will also trigger more fire-fighting.

If you think about your own needs for strategic thinking, how much should you be doing, when should you be doing it, and to what should you be turning your attention? A typical answer adopted by the many people that I coach in senior jobs is to allocate two or more hours a week to these topics. The subjects for strategic thought are updated and planned as part of the process. Here are examples:

- Changing communication strategies

- Career plans

- Internal marketing

- Alliances

- Organizational development

- Support and resources for my team

- Succession planning.

Many of the people I work with on a 1-2-1 basis leave our coaching sessions with diary entries for the whole year blocked out for 'Planning', 'Strategic Development' or other appropriate phrase that suits the culture. They have commitment from their secretaries to book appropriate spaces for this work and to protect those spaces from being regularly captured by others.

Busy heads

Beware the busy head. It can feel great to be active, vital, moving toward goals but this activity, while useful, has not been successful if you look back on any day and think that you did nothing that will look after the needs of your business in six months time or longer. And if you reflect on your day and find that many of your intentions remain unfinished, then the thrill of being busy has reduced your effectiveness.

Leadership demands that we manage our time more effectively. It demands that we understand and act on our personal choices for what we do, how we do it and when we do it. Until we master this thinking and action for ourselves, we are unlikely to be wholly effective in managing those who are different from us in their methods of working and motivation.

The step back

'Step back' is a quick method of gaining objectivity. We have discussed the use of widening the focus in relation to the lock-in syndrome, and 'step back' is another device for checking our mental state and determining whether we are doing as well as we can on any given assignment.

When we notice the signs of fire-fighting, it is helpful to think 'step back'. If you can do this and literally 'step back' then the physical act provides bio-feedback to enhance the effect.

In any case, the pause should be enough to provide a space in which you can ask yourself questions and start some productive processing that will change the way in which you are working. Questions might include:

- Is this the best use of my time now?

- Can I bring other resources to this?

- Is there a more effective way of achieving the actual objective?

- What is most important both now and after completing this task?

Devise your own questions, or adapt these to have the same impact.

Busy bodies

A small number of executives at all levels believe that looking busy makes them appear important. Sadly, this is seldom true; many people are not impressed. In any case, being busy does not have a relationship with good leadership. The executive who cannot flex his diary to meet with staff is not really doing his job. Being late for meetings, making and taking cellphone calls at every opportunity, and walking quickly from one appointment to another may show high activity but they do not raise confidence in those who know what real leadership should be.

Whether the reason for being busy is a misguided status thing or whether there is an inability to prioritize or manage adequately, the busy body needs to be slowed down – it's time to prioritize, to think where our contribution is most needed and to be effective, and how to support our role more adequately, if necessary. Continuing the busy body syndrome is not a sensible option.

As a matter of interest, I once worked for an American business in which people in its large European operation moved so rapidly around the building that they looked as if they were in a mad walking race. In the US holding company people moved around much more slowly. The difference was enormous. Business was not more relaxed in the USA; it was just that overseas everyone dashed around twice as fast. I decided to ignore that local culture when in the European business, but it took an effort of will not to be caught up in the tide. I have no idea whether it was culturally driven (it was actually a multiracial outfit) or caffeine driven.

Do your people move alertly but in a measured way? Or do they dart about like cats in headlights?

Focus on impact

'The misfortunes hardest to bear are those which never come'
JAMES RUSSELL LOWELL

I have adapted the circles of influence and concern (Figure 1.2) from the work of Stephen Covey (1990)[2] and applied it suc-

---

[2] Habit #1: Be proactive.

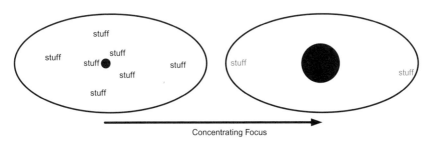

Figure 1.2 Focus for efficacy

cessfully in my coaching and training work with managers and leaders. The model suggests that mental activity is often wasted due to lack of focus and, further, when that happens, the focus should be applied where it will have impact in the world of work.

When we concentrate on 'stuff' that just exists in our work culture but over which, on reflection, we have no chance of effective impact, then we are not being effective. It is wasted time. When we notice ourselves and others doing this, we need to refocus on an area where we do have impact. These simple acts of letting go and refocusing for impact have a fantastic effect – within seconds the 'stuff' is no longer in the picture and we are suddenly being more effective again.

These two steps do depend on having done, at some time, some reflective work on whether the 'stuff' issue (however important emotionally) is something that you can sensibly change. And if there is a chance of doing that, will it be without diminishing your energy for productive work or damaging your status? These are important questions and the answers should determine your action.

The suggestion to refocus on impactful actions seems counter to the measures for getting out of the lock-in syndrome (LIS) where focus is tightly upon work and I advised the use of a wider picture to gain perspective. The biggest difference is that in LIS the focus is roving from one fire to the next without a pause. In that case we need then to widen the focus to gain perspective. Here, we are using focus to counter the effect of unproductive extracurricular thoughts to enable us to become productive again. In many organizations, there are groups of people who continually reiterate the same complaints and trigger other members of their kind to adopt well-rehearsed expressions of helplessness and complaint. Phrases that trigger these unproductive conversations often include:

- HR has no productive benefit at all, in fact the reverse.

- IT again, they can't fix anything without messing up something else.

- Forget it, Facilities Management will just keep you waiting for a year or more.

- Learning & Development haven't a clue what they are doing.

When people spend their time repeating the same, familiar complaints they are contributing toward a growing culture of **we can't** rather than **we can**. By wasting time on conversations without action and any intention of making a difference, each individual is reducing his own energy for success. Focus on action and success, and the complaints disappear.

Being and doing

Another influence of whether we fire-fight or not depends upon our sense of our contribution to the organization. If our sense of impact in the organization is tied up principally with actions, then our sense of work-identity can be weakened if we relinquish our responsibilities (and actions). If our sense of influence goes wider than our actions, we will be more resilient. We will be less likely to be affected if we are given a reduced scope for decisions and action, for example. If we are to contribute more to the long-term health of our organization, then there has to be a tendency to be more active in other, strategic ways to create sustainable futures.

We will return to the subject of 'personal contribution' in Part Three, and here it may be useful to think about the personal pros and cons of letting go of specific responsibilities.

PROS AND CONS OF LETTING GO

Why not make an action list now of things that you feel ready to relinquish, delegate or drop completely?

ACTIONS

Let's now test and flex another critical ability of leaders: that of extended perception.

Extended perception

Having worked out what you need to delegate and what you need to drop completely, imagine, if you will, that you are taking the actions now and that the clock is spinning forward. The outcomes are happening, your workload is less, and your days are less busy on average. What are you doing in your days and what is this experience like now? Is your job more satisfying to you now, or less?

WHAT IS THIS EXPERIENCE LIKE NOW?

Running through such a scenario as if it is happening now is often called 'future pacing'. I call the process a *sensory journey*. The sensory journey is a journey into the future and each journey helps one to gain greater perspective. We miss that perspective if we spend all our time being active in the present. The objective of the sensory journey is to gather more information; the additional perspectives help us to make better, sustainable decisions that work *with* our personal motivations (and needs) rather than *against* them.

Viv works in school education. His workload was enormous. He often worked days of 18 hours and most of his meals were taken away from home, including breakfast and dinner. He rarely saw his children except at weekends. Even that leisure time was interrupted. After going through a process of recalibration and deciding upon actions, he constructed a plan of changes in the school's district administration. When asked to make a sensory journey,[3] he imagined the clock spinning forward very fast. Sometimes he would slow it down again while he took in information about the scenario he was engaged in. He would notice things, people, sounds and light. Then he would let the clock spin forward again. In this sensory journey process Viv discovered that he was very uncomfortable with passing on two of the annual conferences that were a regular feature of his year. Invariably these took place in fabulous locations and provided an opportunity to network, share experiences and learn from the experiences of others in

---

[3] A sensory journey (or future-pacing) is simply the act of imagining being in a future moment as if it was really happening now. This can check that the mindset you have is sufficiently positive and can provide confidence and motivation to succeed.

similar roles. They also provided an opportunity to relax and widen the picture of what is possible. Of his own volition he used the same sensory journey process to imagine being at one of the upcoming conferences and, while there, sharing some of his strategic thinking (for corporate culture change) with a number of colleagues from another State. He determined to reconsider this aspect of 'letting-go' and decided to keep the two particular conferences on his agenda. Viv took two further steps: the first was to free up more time to help with this retention of tasks, and the second was to go on another sensory journey to check that these new areas for letting-go could be integrated into his future way of working – with a positive outcome for him as well as for the administration.

Silent time for reflection

'And in much of your talking, thinking is half murdered'
KAHLIL GIBRAN

There is another use of time that may sound counter-intuitive to productive working – it is that of still space, or silence. Reflective thought is enormously helpful and the benefits are obvious when we think about it – we become more strategic and can see the wider, holistic implications of our actions. So what is this stillness stuff? Stillness is the opposite of the busy head state. There is a spectrum of mental activity that ranges from rapid, logical processing to quiet, low-level being. Figure 1.3 shows the Psychological Stillness–Activity Dimension.

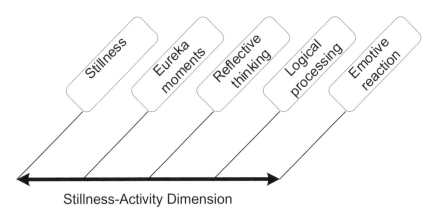

Figure 1.3 Stillness–Activity Dimension

What is your range? Would it be useful to extend the range? If we are to use our skills, flexibly, from logical tasking (busy head) to reflective thought and even further, then a quantum leap is obtained, even to the level of genius. In order to make that more likely it is helpful to exercise our minds to the full limit of our potential. This is similar to a physical workout for the mind. You cannot be comfortable at any level of sustained physical work unless you have worked harder in training. It is the same with our minds; we need to flex and test our minds to explore more widely than we do already so that our range of competence is extended. The methodology for this is similar to strategies for meditation or sleeping, and we all know how to sleep – or do we?

First, switch your attention to noticing your breathing **or** heartbeat. By concentrating on **one** new internal object, the externals fade away. An example in daily life might be the experience of listening to the radio while driving a vehicle. Something happens outside to challenge you and what you were listening to on the radio has gone without your notice. It is only later, when safe, that you realize that you have missed everything that went before. People who use hands-off cell phones while driving on major roads are three times more likely to have accidents than non-phone users. The statistic for those handling the phones may be worse than that!

Spend some minutes to become as calmly concentrated as you can. Now let your awareness of your breathing or your heart-beat diminish. If a thought or observation comes into your mind, allow it to fade away. If you find images coming into your consciousness, let them shrink and drift away into darkness. If there are sounds, allow them to fade too, and maintain this calm attitude of letting everything else go. Physically your breathing will slow and become increasingly shallow.

Stilling the mind in this way increases conscious dominion over your 'personal state'[4] as well as extending your competence in the dimension of mental activity. Now let's consider the far right of the stillness–activity dimension.

Road-rage at work!

You can see that emotive reaction is at the busy end of the dimension in Figure 1.3. Emotional reactions are not wholly cognitive; the bulk of emotional reactivity happens in the mid-brain rather than in the processing higher-brain, the cere-

---

[4]By personal state I mean psychological state. We have many of them, not one. Some of us are able to decide on our state, others have little or no control and simply respond to stimuli, often in highly predictable ways.

brum. Importantly, the mid-brain processes about 8,000 times faster than the higher, logical brain. Why is that interesting? Think of colleagues who get very aggressive or over-expressive in meetings? Think of road-rage at the extreme of behaviors. When the mid-brain takes control, it takes a successful, patterned mental adaptation to stop the roller-coaster!

Such emotional responses are normal, commonplace and largely go unnoticed at the less extreme responses. For example, if you or a colleague sometimes experience intense anger in meetings and hence miss a large part of the dialogue as a result (of 'going internal'), then you now know why that is. The mid-brain has taken over and left the highest logical processing behind. A success strategy to change that might also be useful too; so let's take a look at the emotive impact curve in Figure 1.4.

The diagram represents the effect of a comment or event that creates a mid-brain, emotive reaction. The level of impact may follow a typical course like that shown in the dashed line. The person experiences a trigger (T) that may be a

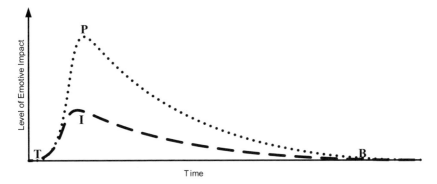

Figure 1.4 Emotive impact curve

comment, observation or physical event. The person 'goes internal' and there may or may not be a series of processing checks and thoughts that kick in after the initial rise (dotted curve).[5] If lucky, the impact will not go sky-high, but will reach an early peak (P) and mellow out until the base level (B) is again reached. During this period, the individual can then slowly increase his or her attention on what is happening externally again. Sometimes there is a sinusoidal effect rather than a slow down-curve, creating waves of emotional impact and also sometimes reaction – inappropriate anger, verbal abuses, and so forth. Hormones are also affected when there are greater levels of emotive impact, and the slow removal of these by the liver and kidneys can make the process of recovery even longer.

In order to head-off the emotional responses, it is necessary to notice the earliest possible part of the response pattern and make an intervention (I) that will ameliorate the effects, as shown on the dashed curve. For maximum effect, the intervention needs to be a question. It might also be an event that breaks the installed pattern[6] or initiates a more useful (learned pattern of response[7]). The simplest method, naturally enough, is to ask an internal question such as:

---

[5] This is analogous to the chaining of events in patterned behaviors discussed earlier.

[6] Many people will be familiar with the use of an elastic band worn on the wrist in order to help to break unwanted patterns. Similar thinking is used in the training of animals.

[7] I am referring here to the method of establishing 'anchors'. Anchors are learned patterns that are positive. These anchored patterns can easily be linked to 'negative' triggers in order to break existing patterns and automatically replace them with a useful one. The methodology for this can be found in a number of NLP books and in McLeod (2003).

- What is really happening here now?

- Is a response needed now or later?

- What would be the most professional attitude to adopt right now?

In asking and then answering questions like these, our attention creates increased activity in the cerebrum; we start thinking logically again. The effects of the mid-brain are reduced over time!

Because the mid-brain is so fast, the question will invariably be someway up the emotive impact curve. It's a steep curve, so the question needs to be short, fast and early! In coaching people, we ask them what they first notice when they experience these events. Here is a typical dialogue:

Angus: *So, what do you first notice when this pattern starts?*
Coachee: *My head starts to throb.*
Angus: *And if something happens just before that throb, what is that thing that happens just before?*
Coachee: *It's like there is a freezing of time for a millisecond and a cold blade opens up my forehead.*
Angus: *And if something happens just before that freezing and the cold blade opens up 'my forehead', what is that thing that happens just before that freezing?*

In practice, the longer the pattern has been experienced, the more the number of levels of experience one typically finds. It is quite common to discover 20 levels of experience, all of them happening within an instant. I note these on a timeline, all of them falling on the first part of the impact curve. Generally, the longer period of time over which the individual has had the pattern, the more details one finds when unpacking it.

The questioning above is designed to help the coachee to stay deeply in the discovery process. As you can see, the words that are expressed are reflected back as perfectly as possible, so there is no need to translate them. It is like a keyhole that lets words (the key) out and then I insert my key (the coachee's reflected words) – my key slots right back in again without any resistance. The coachee does not notice or question the words because those are the words the coachee used. Because this process of reflective-questioning is so perfect for the keyhole, the coachee does not notice the construction of the sentences[8] either. The coachee is able to stay with his or her own evolutionary thinking and discovery in an exquisite way.

---

[8] A systematic approach is that of Symbolic Modeling, identified in the excellent and effective work of Lawley and Tompkins (2000).

2

Life balance

MOST EXECUTIVES HAVE DEMANDING JOBS SO WE HAVE good excuses for being late for friends, children and spouses. We have good excuses for being distracted at home and good excuses for not really being present in family life. Nothing changes unless we revalue, and not all of us want to. However, if things are not as you would wish, there is always scope for improvement if we apply a higher level of directed attention to all the issues.

In any event, it is worth questioning whether excessive time at work over the mid- or long-term is actually efficient. Logic and experience suggests that persistently high levels of work-time increases the incidence and severity of errors and reduces efficacy. If you happen to be experiencing lock-in syndrome then you would not have the clarity to have this perception!

One of the problems about addressing attention to life-balance is also due to the effects of lock-in syndrome (or of fire-fighting at the lesser level). We get so focused that the rest of our needs (and those of others) get sidelined. To make changes we must take the time to investigate the issues properly, not curtail the process by following existing patterns. Making snap decisions is unlikely to create a solution if it is those snap decisions that caused the problems in the first place! For those that have the desire and will to change, the following section looks at the evaluation of life-balance and strategies for making positive differences in the short and long term.

Where there is a will, there is a way

When we consider life-balance it is helpful to set up some areas for introspection. Here is a typical list:

- Friends

- Rest and holidays

- Eating out

- Physical activity

- Health

- Wealth

- Appearance

- Hobbies

- Kids

- Family life

- Partnership

- Personal growth

- Faith activities

- Contribution to others

- Environment of home.

A good first step is to identify the present position and decide what you would like it to be. In Figure 2.1, the Life-Balance executive has set down five main elements for consideration. In each, he has placed his ranking out of a possible 10, for 'my comfort rating with the current situation' and, his ranking for 'my desired comfort rating in two months'. Thus, for 'Friends

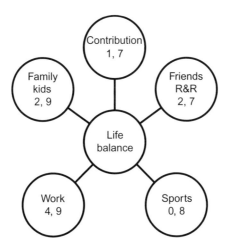

Figure 2.1   Present and desired rankings for key life balance issues

R&R' his current ranking is 2 but he desires to reach a level of 7 out of a possible 10. Each individual will focus on what is especially important to him alone.

In every case there was scope for improvement, in some cases massive improvement – if only he could find the time. In questioning, I learned that his dissatisfaction with work was not due to lack of commitment or interest, just unhappiness that the rest of his life was a footnote to work. He was no longer involved in any sports although he had been a Karate Blue at University. He had also put on weight. He had already missed too many of his children's firsts: league matches, first classes and stage appearances. He had been involved in coaching the under-12's football, but no longer. And most of his rest and recuperation (R&R) time was 'recovery time' without social contact of any memorable value.

What, in these circumstances, are your categories and how would you rank your levels now and your desired levels, 0 to 10?

CATEGORIES AND RATINGS NOW AND DESIRED? TIME SCALE FOR CHANGE?

Finding time

What time commitments have to change to make your objectives real? After juggling, invariably there are quite a number of hours to be found! Let's investigate many of the factors that impact on your time and give attention to each. What can be saved? How? When can that be done? How much time do you want to save?

- Core needs of my talent

- Tertiary needs that others should do

- Travel time to and from work

- Overseas engagements

- Inland travel

- Extracurricular corporate activity

- Regular, rolling meetings

- Main office location

- Secondary office location

- Days working from home

- Booking uninterrupted space for thinking

- Management skills of my reports

- Training needs of my reports

- Support needs for my team

- Communication methods

- Reporting actually required (and formats)

- Other extraneous jobs and functions

- Sign-offs, checking

- Presentations – who creates and delivers

- Projects that could be off-loaded

- Training and support for delegation

- Who do I over-manage (See Part Two)

- Add others.

Each change will need a time-frame, and most changes will impact elsewhere, so you will also need to consider, holistically, the impact of changes and communicate to those affected in a way that fits with the needs of the organization (see Part Two).

ACTIONS

Most people begin to see multiple areas where they can reduce their time-efforts without negatively affecting their productivity. Often, restructuring some of these activities is more productive. Delegation can help juniors to step up to the plate and achieve at a higher level. People who fail in restructuring and delegation are often neurotic, that is, feeling overly responsible for the things that should not concern them. Sometimes their issue relates to their need to feel in control or a drive to own or be associated directly with all forward movement. These people often need outside help to gain perspective and or improve their sense of self-worth.

If you have not already done so, please calculate the expected savings in time and the extent of any gap by comparing the actual saving you have identified with the extra time you needed to find.

If there is still a gap, ask yourself whether this compromise is acceptable in the short term. If it is not, then it may be worthwhile revisiting the list above. What other area of time can you identify that is not already in your list? Be tougher on yourself and go through the system again. Be cool and calculated.

When you have found more time, it is still important to consider the holistic impacts of change before making commitments. Remember to take a sensory journey (often known as 'future pacing') to imagine what it is like now (to have made those decisions), informed those people and to be doing things differently. If that is a positive experience and is holistically sound, then you have probably already made a commitment to those changes.

Honoring jobs done

One of the essential traits of leaders is the ability to pause after most of their successes and give personal credit for the job done. The Healthy Action Cycle can be seen in Figure 2.2.

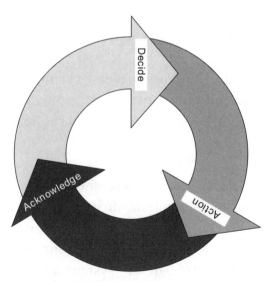

Figure 2.2 Healthy Action Cycle

This may sound a little immodest, but it is important. Firstly, if we give ourselves realistic credit, we are then less dependent on feedback from others. Secondly, if we do not pause for acknowledgment we are very likely to suffer the lock-in syndrome and move too rapidly to the next decision. There are times for those behaviors but they have dangers, as we have already seen. Let me express the true tale of a friend.

Robin was a high-achiever. He was the Marketing Director of one of the best known national monuments in the world. He wrote a regular column for a pre-eminent specialist journal on guns, and was a regular contributor to other journals. He had enjoyed a fine military career in a prestigious, world-famous regiment. He was also one of the funniest and most well-connected people I ever met. He was self-effacing and his extraordinary achievements and background were only learned by others, quietly, over some years. He knew most of the first and second rank of the British Royal family through his social standing. An evening with Robin meant that we would be laughing the whole time while he told jokes and stories and imitated famous people. We would cry with so much laughing that my jaw would ache. But Robin only knew how to do the first two things in the Healthy Action Cycle, Decide and Action. He was predisposed to be stoical, self-reliant and competent. The last time I saw Robin, I was driving on a stormy winter's day. He was walking along the sidewalk in his local town. A few days later Robin put on a heavy coat, waded into the River Thames, and drowned himself. Tears fell again at his funeral service.

At its most extreme, lack of acknowledgment (and refusal to take seriously the compliments of others) can result in clinical depression. There are, of course, shades of gray in the extent to which we self-acknowledge. The Healthy Action Cycle model suggests that we should be doing some of it, some of the time at least! Acknowledgment helps to create self-esteem and self-confidence and these then generate the potential for making bigger steps later on. Self-acknowledgment is one key to that journey. We will look at the application of this learning when managing others in Part Two.

3

Personal goals

WE HAVE ALREADY STARTED THE PROCESS OF establishing goals and it would be wrong to leave out a short section on goal theory, in spite of the fact that hardly any manager alive does not know at least one model for goal-setting. Here I wish briefly to encapsulate the basics and add something that is rarely addressed, but I believe should be.

We have established that we are mostly too busy to enjoy a really healthy, balanced life. So when approaching any goal, it is worth preceding the standard processes with the pre-goal method.

The pre-goal method

1. Is this goal important enough to commit to now?

2. What level of time and resource commitments are likely to be needed?

3. Do I have the time and resources available for this goal?

4. What else can be removed from my action list to make space for this new goal?

Questions 2 and 3 both refer to 'resources'. Resource needs will include emotional factors that drive or hinder forward movement. For example, if you happen to be feeling tired or running out of energy, then commiting yourself to another action will not make you more successful. First, it may be necessary to make another decision about commitments, or the timing of those commitments. Only when space is left for energy is it reasonable to add any more actions.

The pre-goal questions check whether the goal should be on the agenda at all. Further, it makes sure that less important things are removed from the list in order to boost the resources available for success.

The idea for this came through watching people coach one another at professional coach-training events. Time after time, coaches would encourage their coachees to establish so-called 'well-formed' goals without first checking whether the coachee really had the resources to accomplish the goal, whatever their initial level of motivation and commitment. I started to doubt whether some of the standard methods of coaching would be successful. I also experienced some of this coaching and found that my committed actions sometimes fell out of sight by the time I was supposed to have completed my tasks. For me, Question 4, 'What else can be removed from my action list to make space for this new goal?' was a key factor in coaching to goals from that point onward.

Once the pre-goal conditions are satisfied, any of the standard methods for well-formed goals[1] can be applied. Whatever model you use, they are likely to include some or all of the following.

Goal conditions

The most frequently applied goal conditions include attention to the following factors:

1. Specific and clearly stated

2. Within personal control

3. Positive effect

4. Significant impact

5. Needs a significant level of 'stretch' to achieve

6. Definable outcome

7. Achievable

8. Holistically satisfactory[2] (tertiary effects on self and others in achieving the goal are satisfactory)

---

[1] Strictly-speaking, well-formed goals should embrace all aspects of my pre-goal method – it is only because the practice of forming them is often poor that I wish to focus on those factors that are critical (and most often neglected) in order to redress the balance.
[2] This check is sometimes called an 'ecology check'.

9. Time-constrained

10. Mile posts applied (for larger goals with a number of sub-tasks).

Of course, at each mile post and at the end, it is worth considering the use of the Healthy Action Cycle to acknowledge the achievement! That boosts both self-esteem and self-confidence and one can then take bigger, more stretching steps next time.

Motivation traits

Another useful way of checking motivation in respect of goals involves the identification of four 'motivation traits'.[3] Take a look at any goal to which you have made a commitment, but not yet attempted. If it is not already written down, please do so now.

MY GOAL

---

[3] The four 'motivation traits' were identified by Rose Charvet (1997) from over 80 human traits called metaprograms.

Having written out the goal, see if you can identify the following four factors:

1. Language suggesting a 'toward orientation' rather than 'prevention of something unwanted' ('away from' language)

2. Language indicating that the goal is internalized and resourced by personal drive and not that of others.

3. Language that suggests a procedural process without any alternative options.

4. Language that is all stated positively, not negatively.

Here are some examples, together with their opposites:

- I want us to gain that national status.

  I do not wish to fall into the same trap again.

- I feel committed to this result.

  I am motivated by Tom's belief in this objective.

- The steps I am going to start taking are . . .

  I will start with a report or a presentation to Board . . .

- Gaining this award will be a tremendous boost for us.

  If we do not get national status our market may diminish.

If all these conditions are met, the chance of success is high. If any are missing or the opposite is stated, the chance of success is lower. In this case it may be worth asking more questions about the goal and whether, after all, it is worthy of your attention. This may enable you to recalibrate its importance and modify, delete or find greater commitment to the goal and its achievement.

Do the following meet the four criteria?

> *When Peter is well again, I will arrange a meeting with his secretary and talk with him about my career advancement aspirations. I will ask for his support.*

An issue here that does not satisfy is the proviso that Peter must be well. How well must he be? What control is there that he will ever be 'well enough'? A motivated statement might read better:

> *Peter is currently off sick and so I cannot sensibly engage with him about my career aspirations but that gives me a good reason to speak with his VP and ask her advice so I will continue to call round to her office until she is available to see me.*

The Stretch Zone

'Our deepest fear is not that we are inadequate. Our deepest fear is that we are powerful beyond measure'

MARIANNE WILLIAMSON[4]

---

[4] This quotation is more often associated with the inaugural speech of Nelson Mandela as President in 1994 but was written by Marianne Williamson.

The Stretch Zone sits outside our Comfort Zone. When we are in the Comfort Zone we are reacting easily to events and using lots of patterned responses to familiar scenarios. When we are psychologically challenged, whether intellectually or emotionally, we move into the Stretch Zone, which is also known as the Learning Zone. For goals to have your increased confidence and be inspiring enough to have your commitment, it is important that they can create a significant stretch for you. The phrase, 'for you' is critical. What works for me cannot be projected onto someone else. It follows that as managers we must not make similar assumptions about what a stretch is for each of our people – we must ask each of them.

So what is 'stretch'? The Stretch Zone (Figure 3.1) is characterized by resistance. At worst, it is characterized by paralysis

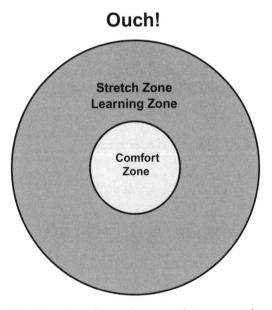

Figure 3.1 Stretch to learn: from comfort to stretch zones

of action. Resistance may be triggered by a limiting belief[5] about one's competence to achieve. It is always driven by emotional factors and typically the overriding emotion is fear.

There are invariably two factors in our limitations: our logical thinking about the consequences (often wrong), and our emotional resistance. To increase our effectiveness we need to check out both factors and address them. Our logical thinking can be challenged by asking questions that demand new perspectives to what we have been thinking or imagining.

- Who says that I will fail?

- When have I felt similarly but succeeded?

- What have others done and how did they achieve?

- What other resources can I muster to help me do this?

- So, 43 percent fail. What are the characteristics of the 57 percent who succeed?

- How can I counter that weakness?

- How can I augment that strength?

Our emotional concerns need primarily to be acknowledged, and one of the most useful things to do is then to ask yourself,

---

[5] Limiting beliefs are those concepts that we hold to be true even though they have a debilitating effect on our enjoyment or performance.

'So what?' Invariably the first part, acknowledgment, works like magic. Once you name the dragon, it is tangible only for a few seconds and then fades, as the quotation runs: 'the misfortunes hardest to bear are those that never come.'

- Why shouldn't I feel worried? This is a big deal. So what?

The leader will make sure that the balance between comfort and stretch in both their work and personal development is healthy. Unless some disaster befalls, the leader wants to be sure that there is stability and comfort in their life irrespective of what is happening at work and at home. This self-preservation at all costs provides the greater sense of balance and reason.

The leader is also a developing individual, not just an expert who has arrived. Therefore, the level of stretch and learning that the leader embraces is likely to be significantly higher than for most managers. The leader is used to the process of gauging risks, taking them and succeeding, and that leads to a mentality (or mindset[6]) of performance at the next level.

---

[6] A mindset is simply a set of values, beliefs and a sense of self that help (or hinder) us in a given situation. We will refer to these again later.

4

Wheel of work

THE WHEEL OF WORK IS SIMILAR TO THE LIFE BALANCE wheel but here the object is to focus on the world of work and aspects of it that determine our level of satisfaction at work. You can design your own wheel, but it is likely to contain some of the segments shown in Figure 4.1.

Segments of the wheel

Let's quickly run through each segment to add some color to these simple descriptors. I have written the text as if it applies to a member of your own staff since we will return to the use of the wheel in this context later.

Reward and recognition (R&R)

Rewards are the benefits package including bonuses. Recognition is about the soft-stuff that feeds back to us from

My Contentment Level with...

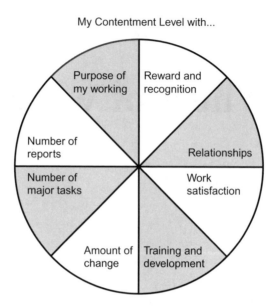

Figure 4.1 Typical Wheel of Work

colleagues and stakeholders and provides a sense of belonging, purpose, value or self-fulfillment. For this and all the other segments the question is, 'What is your contentment level?' The answers need to provide both of you with information about the relative importance of R&R compared to other aspects of the job. Since everyone is different, a narrow set of parameters will not satisfy the majority. We need to be flexible to accommodate that fact. It is also helpful to develop people's highest possible enjoyment of their working life so that they broaden their exposure to sources of gratification and the recognition that can bring them. For example, someone with extracurricular team skills at a club may be able to use some of those same skills within the business. If they do this, it may provide them with an opportunity for acknowledgment and bring together otherwise entirely separate aspects of their life. Analytical Graphics, Malvern in PA, provides laundry services at work and free meals for visiting families, every day. Their motivation is to reduce the issues in managing some of the tasks that are normally squeezed in between work and home. Naturally the workers there feel valued and the company is one of the top 25 employers in the USA.

Relationships

The context for all these questions is work, so we are seeking to define, on balance, how content the person is with those relationships at work. Relationships create some of the most important motivations and demotivations in the workplace. Failure to address issues can very seriously affect the wellbeing and health of employees, quite apart from the reduction in their productive ability as individuals or within a team context. If we help them to resolve such issues we will improve our own relationship with the individuals as well as gain from their rising contentment at work.

Work satisfaction

These are the other intangibles that might make one feel more or less happy to return to the same job and organization. One person may hate the air-conditioning or the lack of daylight; another may dislike the distraction of a view. One person may wish to make many decisions in the day about what he does and when he does it; another person will prefer to have an ordered structure for her day. Some people are distracted by a peaceful view or like their days to be well-ordered before they come into work. Each of these factors, and more, will be very specific to each individual. When asking about job satisfaction, remember to also ask the opposing question:

> *Tom, is there anything else that you are dissatisfied with where I might help or have impact?*

If we expect the answers to be a can of worms then they most likely will be. If, however, we adjust our mindset to one of facilitating contentment in the person, then the results are likely to be more useful. We help that outcome by focusing on areas where they can make the most impact. We achieve that most productively by asking questions rather than by talking or giving advice.

Training and development

How content are the individuals with the level of training and development exposure they have? Are they almost fully able to do every aspect of their current role? What about the next job? Are they already positioned for a move and do they already have the skills and qualifications necessary for that next post? A leader is never fearful of the aspirations of their staff members and will get more from them by helping them to become as capable as they can be. We all know managers who resist the talent and aspirations of people below them because it threatens their stability. Leaders have no time for such restricted ideas.

Amount of change

Some people may like a lot of change at work and see them as acceptable challenges. Or they may be tired of changes and want some stability. They may also dislike the extent of changes that come from elsewhere and over which they have limited or no control. Their work may or may not contain sufficient variety or not allow them to concentrate and become expert in a field of their choice. In leading people we are mindful of the dynamic between the benefits of 'security' aspects[1] (familiarity, consistency, status quo) and the learning that comes from the Stretch Zone. Be open, specific and ask them what would be a stretch for them in terms of change? Would that be helpful to them? Conversations along these lines will open up the discussion and reveal other areas where, at no cost, we can make a significant difference to the productive commitment of some of our people.

Number of major tasks

Most people have an idea how many major tasks are ideal for them to manage. Some like one major project in which they get totally absorbed, feel most expert and feel most valuable. Others get bored easily or want a spread of activity. How many do they have, and is this number too few or too many for them to cope with? We may not be able to do anything immediately but we should be able to accommodate their wishes in the mid-term, even if it means moving or up-

---

[1] The use of the word 'security' with this meaning will be familiar to those exposed to the work of Maslow (1943).

skilling them to work in another area. Another question you may prefer to use is:

> *Tom, how content are you with the level of responsibility you have at work?*

This question may also lead to, or cover, the following segment.

Number of reports

How many people report to them directly or indirectly? Are there too many or too few to manage successfully? We discussed this issue earlier and it can be central to performance. Discussion about numbers may lead to discussion about the actual skill level of the reporting staff and their development or some restructuring to up-skill in their area. Questions may arise about merging certain functions for greater control and effectiveness.

Purpose of my working

What are the key factors that make a person's purpose in work most worthwhile and how content are they with the status quo compared to each of those factors?

People are amazingly different and your answers to this and all these questions are likely to be absolutely unique. Later we will look at some of these different motivations, but, currently, what is your personal purpose in working? What factors are most important to you, and to what extent can you change the situation to enhance your pleasure of the work experience overall?

When ranking, you can use the process of allocating values from 0 (low) to 10 range. Having ranked all your segments, ask yourself how high might be your maximum rank in each case? The reason for this question is because many people never rank 10 for anything (even if you provide a range of 10, as above). Instead they have an in-built limit of 9, 8 or 7 for example. Having established your maximum (and if appropriate, your minimum) to arrive at a potential range, check out each rank against the range. Where can you make realistic changes that impact on your level of satisfaction overall?

If you have limits in your power and control over certain areas, does this commit you to changing? What can you achieve and where might you compromise? Can you establish a plan, within a time-frame, for change?

Typically, people find two or three areas that make the most impact, then concentrate on establishing actions in those areas. In each case, remember the pre-goal questions and make sure that the goals are all well formed.

ACTIONS

5

Solution thinking

W^E ARE REPEATEDLY MAKING DECISIONS AND providing solutions. Some of these (for example, type A in Figure 5.1) are almost instinctive: learned, patterned responses to familiar scenarios. Our minds recognize certain patterns and create patterned responses because the automatic process is efficient and fast. However, dangers also lurk there. Quick solutions are not always the best.

Other solutions (type B in the figure) take more time to resolve,[1] while type-C solutions are often beneficial for more difficult issues that require effective results. Typically, these issues take more resources, research, dialog, thinking-through scenarios and checking out the holistic impact of each potential solution.

---

[1] Indeed, we may put some of these off, hoping that the need to find a solution may become less important and thus slip off the list.

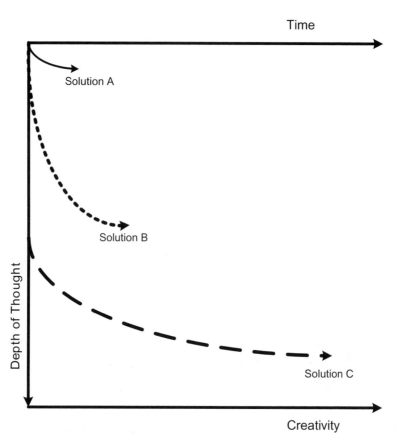

Figure 5.1 Deep Thought and creativity

All of these solution processes are within the orbit of management and good personal leadership. Much of what we create by way of solutions will be determined by our experience, our successes and failures. What is clear is that sometimes the need for an innovative and effective solution is lost because we react too quickly from experience, without thinking through or thinking deeply enough. Clearly if one solution is adequate for the job, then there is little point in spending a lot of time finding another. Occasionally, a goal is more significant and we recognize that the solution could be different and more cost-effective, for example. Type-C solutions are needed when an organization has produced similar business plans over several years and has failed to achieve their objectives. Type-C solutions are needed, for example, when years of culture change initiatives have failed to make any significant difference. In these cases, how do we arrive at type-C solutions? First, it is helpful to put aside a period of time that reflects the importance of finding a good solution.

It is clear that greater time is involved in exploring an increasing number of options, extending novelty or thinking 'outside the box'. Our inclination as decision-makers may be to short-circuit the process and mainly deal in the realm of type-A solutions. On balance then, as leaders, it may occasionally be useful to seek type-B and type-C solutions. As mentioned previously, it is only through exercising the mind that a wider range of choices can be available to us.

Deep Thought solutions

In order to have Deep Thought, it is necessary to suspend judgment. This part of the Deep Thought process is familiar to those who have used the methods of brainstorming. Brainstorming involves retrieving information quickly from a number of people and having someone else capture the thoughts. Judgments are not allowed at this stage. Deep Thought is similar in that judgments are suspended also. The brainstorming scenario is a useful first base in arriving at more options and more creative solutions in Deep Thought.

At its most basic, one can just write down thoughts and solutions without judgment. However, Deep Thought can be enhanced by an adapted process whereby judgments are still suspended, but time is given for quiet reflection. In brainstorming with groups, so much information is typically set down that nobody thinks to slow the process and have quiet reflection in order to find further solutions. It is only when there are very few ideas on the page that quiet introspection may be allowed to take place. In Deep Thought we are determined to wait for fresh ideas.[2] We can also use positive inducers of creative thought; questions that suggest that there is another answer, even though we do not (yet) know what that answer is. A typical inducer-question is,[3] 'If there is a very different way of looking at this, what is that very different way?'

We have talked already about having (time) spaces for reflective and strategic thinking and planning. For Deep Thought solutions, it is important to take a complete break and come back to the issue later. These breaks need only be for some minutes, and taken in silence. The same rules apply for Deep Thought solutions in groups. With complex issues it may be necessary to leave longer spaces and time-table a sequence of actual meetings.

History informs us that a great deal of major discovery has taken place after periods of deep thinking followed by rest. A novel solution then suddenly pops up. A famous example is

---

[2] The U-model is a similar device involving a three-part process: sensing, presencing and realizing, see Senge et al. (2004).
[3] Sometimes called 'unblocking questions'.

that of Archimedes in his bath, forming the principle that a body completely or partially submerged in a fluid is acted upon by an upward force which is equal to the weight of the fluid displaced by the body. This was his 'Eureka' moment. Then there was Kékulé who had racked his brains unsuccessfully to understand why his hydrocarbon chemicals had too little hydrogen associated with them. He was sitting on a bus when, in his daydream, he saw snakes which then ate their own tails – thus he discovered the existence of aromatic, cyclic hydrocarbons as opposed to the familiar, snake-like, long-chain, aliphatic hydrocarbons.

Flexible thinking and the multiple intelligences

'It is not the strongest of the species that survive, nor the most intelligent, but the one most responsive to change'
CHARLES DARWIN

Managers and leaders need more mental agility and a wider range of choices about how they approach things mentally. Leaders are probably more likely to be experienced in using a wider range of psychological skills. We have not yet looked at Emotional Intelligence, which is dealt with in more detail in Part Three. At present, however, please consider this supposition where EQ means emotional quotient and IQ is the more familiar intelligence quotient:

EQ + IQ = Success

The supposition suggests that those who have competences in both these areas of intelligence are more likely to be successful. In simple terms, it ought to be true, at least within egalitarian communities. Those who understand more about the motivations and demotivations of themselves probably understand more about those aspects in others. If that were true, those with higher EQ would generally galvanize more people, more of the time. And those people would work harder and more effectively for them.

While considering these two intelligences, let's consider, briefly, one of several theories about multiple intelligence that is now incorporated into the body of work called 'Accelerated Learning'. Gardner (1983) postulated multiple intelligences, originally proposing these seven:

1. Logical–mathematical

2. Spatial

3. Linguistic

4. Bodily-kinesthetic

5. Musical

6. Intrapersonal

7. Interpersonal.

Intrapersonal intelligence concerns the ability to have useful internal dialogue without irrational, negative self-judgment.

Interpersonal skills have to do largely with the listening and communication skills one applies with others.

You might consider that musical or spatial intelligence may not feature in your management, but these are aspects of mental use that, if developed, have repercussions for the quality of our thinking overall. We are lesser beings and leaders if we are undeveloped in any of our intelligences.

Would an increased ability in any of these seven intelligences improve your effectiveness at work? Which would they be, and what might you do to improve your current ability?

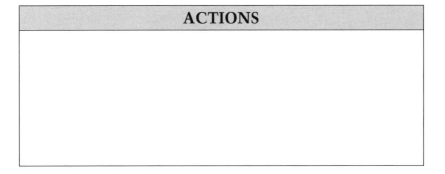

Part of my thinking in asking these questions is to ask you to exercise your psychology before we start to look at leadership as it impacts on others. Later we will also look at Emotional Intelligence and its link with performance at work.

6

Applying personal changes

I HOPE THAT SO FAR I HAVE PROVIDED YOU WITH IDEAS FOR making different approaches in your work. But how will such changes be interpreted by the people who work for you? While any changes you have decided will have obvious benefits for you, sometimes your motives may be misinterpreted. What will staff, colleagues and bosses be thinking when they observe you behaving differently? Sometimes communication is needed to ameliorate misinterpretation there too; a positive-spin also helps!

When considering your boss, if lucky, the area of decision-making will already fit in with a development area that has been noticed and/or agreed at your own 1-2-1. In that case you can simply describe the actions you are taking. Let's consider some examples.

Reducing work time

The reality may be that you have decided to get away from work earlier and set out times for strategic thinking in your diary – no matter how open your diary is to other people. The upshot is that you will be working fewer hours. How can you sell these new behaviors?[1]

Think about the positive things that your boss(es) may observe as benefits, and communicate them.

Tom, I have been too busy with the day-to-day and not spending enough time on the longer-range threats and opportunities, succession plans and opportunities for cost saving. I have started to put that right by working away from the office more so I can take a bigger view. What I hope you will notice in the mid-term is a greater strategic contribution to business development, more innovative solutions and better anticipation of trends. I will also spend extra time with three of my direct reports who need a higher level of support right now. To achieve that I have withdrawn from a number of things that are now running smoothly and no longer need senior control. That should help to develop some of my best people who will be taking over those roles. It's going to encourage wider participation and provide improved back-up if I am overseas. I hope my direct reports will be better at self-starting without me breathing down their necks all the time.

So much time and efficiency is wasted by being too busy. Fire-fighting and the lock-in syndrome are not effective strat-

---

[1] I use the word 'behaviors' to embrace all observable actions in the work context, including mannerisms, assertiveness, speech-patterns, alertness, expressiveness and so on.

egies for productive work. Content people feeling in control of their working days and also feeling that they have prepared enough for upcoming scenarios are much more effective than those who have not.

We often find that the most senior people work less time after being coached. When we review the coaching together we also find that they believe that their contribution and effective status have both increased. This is largely due to the quality of their contributions. They are better at anticipation and better prepared. Those results come from widening their field of attention at the level of strategy, and narrowing their field of attention at the level of purpose.

Part Two

Influence – Leadership of Others

THE BULK OF PART TWO IS CONCERNED WITH A LEADER'S personal impact with others. Leadership is characterized by influencing behaviors and this part of the book is dedicated to understanding the role of the leader as influencer.

If you change the way you work, then that has an impact on some of those who work for you. Leadership involves being aware of this potential and making sure that consistent messages are disseminated. It is important that key people are spoken to on a 1-2-1 basis so that they understand what is happening and why. We will also consider the strategic elements of leadership.

The actions you may have committed to in Part One will necessarily create changes in your behavior and these will be noticed by others around you. Let's revisit our definition of behavior – we mean any observable action in the work context.

That could mean a characteristic or change in many things, for example: self-reflection, planning time, strategic expression, calmness, gravitas, detailed knowledge, awareness and expression of consequences, language patterns, meeting set-up and so on. Any change in these behaviors will be noticed so we will also look at how leaders manage those situations.

In order to generate more ideas for personal impact and to widen understanding about the breadth of action that other leaders have taken, we continue the discussion at the end of Part One.

7

Widening and narrowing attention

I STATED THAT MANY SENIOR EXECUTIVES CAN WORK LESS, BE more effective and boost effective-status at the same time. A key component that produces those results is changing the field of our attention. By that, I mean, firstly, widening strategic attention to new levels and, secondly, narrowing the field of attention at the level of purpose. How does that manifest at work?

In order to create a solution to both of those questions, I propose to detail two further sets of questions. Answer those and clarity should result.

Further questions

Widening the field at the level of strategy

- How can I and the objectives and results of my organization be better appreciated?

- Who do I and my people need to form closer relationships with in order to accelerate our impact?

- Who is against us and what can we do to ameliorate that?

- Who has doubtful allegiance but is a powerful influencer?

- What possible future events and trends might impact on our business?

- How can I get improved cooperation post-merger?

- What restructuring would be useful and what would be the fallout?

- How can I get my people to work as a team?

- Who will I develop to take over aspects of my job and how?

- What ought to remain core to the business in five years' time and what could be contracted out or floated off?

- What expertise must we preserve and develop to keep our added value?

- What contingency plans have we for a plant fire?

Answering these questions and others like them will start to develop potential tactics and actions for change.

Narrowing the field at the level of purpose

- What am I really here to do?

- Where are my skills best applied?

- What can other people do instead of me now?

- What can I drop completely?

- How can I harness my assistants and direct reports to protect me from burning?

Questions like these immediately translate into actions, freeing up time for the extra strategic jobs.

Typical actions

Executives who go through coaching or this type of logical process will invariably commit to many actions. Here are real ones from a wide range of senior executives:

- Create strategic-thinking time; call it 'Development Project' on the calendar and plan ahead for a year at a time.

- Have my assistant book private meeting room spaces for those now.

- Agree diary-entry policy with my secretary to protect spaces.

- Book extra coaching sessions.

- Produce position paper for main Board.

- Create web-based monthly magazine for stakeholders to inform and involve.

- Take team away for two days facilitated discussion on upcoming changes.

- Encourage travel and six-month job-switching between countries to improve collaborative-productivity and improved best-practice worldwide.

- Open second office at our factory near my home; work from there Friday and Monday.

- Meet with shareholders-with-portfolio with remits in my area.

- Meet with European CEO to update on aims for next year.

- Spend time with FD at NY meeting and try to get on the same page.

- Be proactive in setting meetings and running them with my boss.

- Research new technology that may affect our business.

- Have Tom produce and deliver the monthly report to the Board.

- Have our interdivisional report produced by the Project Heads with only a covering introduction from me.

- Channel all unnecessary email to folder with auto-message about not viewing unless there is an expressed requirement for me to do so.

- Withdraw from eight meetings a month, send delegates to three others.

- Have 1-2-1 with all my reports to explain the change in my working pattern and expectations and assess their needs through the change.

In coaching, a large number of such actions invariably result. The advantage of coaching is that perceptions about impact and support for changes can be challenged and worked through, gaining confidence and pace. The coach will challenge your thinking and create unease – the stretch zone where leaps of learning take place.

Changes: overt motives made clear

When we think about changing our behaviors we may consider how acceptable these are in our culture and what others may think. While valuable, these thoughts could cause us to deviate from our purpose. Let's not fall into the trap of weaker managers. Let's counter the negatives with positives, and then decide.

The leader is not afraid to experiment with behaviors but does so wisely, having thought through the consequences. Leaders have a positive mental attitude, focusing on what they can do, rather than on what they cannot. It is worth writing that where new behaviors will be significantly different from before, that a form of communication may be necessary to ensure that the reasons for your behaviors are not misinterpreted. More is said about this later but suffice to give an example. Imagine that one of your new behaviors will be to lessen the over-management of your staff. If you do not explain (and preferably discuss this with them before action) they may interpret your apparent withdrawal in this way:

- He/she has been head-hunted and is on the way out.

- He/she has given-up on me, I'm on my way out.

- My project is a low priority now.

Clearly, misinterpretation cannot be allowed to occur, so the process of discussion, agreement and change needs to happen in that order. We will develop this theme with examples later.

8

Rapport skills and building trust

TRUST IS ESSENTIAL BECAUSE THERE ARE FEW ROLES where performance is only due to one person. Invariably, even if you have no direct or indirect reports, there are people who can make a significant difference. The differences may affect whether you achieve, when you achieve and whether you are still resourced adequately after you have succeeded (in order to take on the next project or aim).

Rapport is an important component in building trust. Two factors are particularly helpful in creating working rapport: (1) being supportive of people and (2) being interested in people (and displaying the behaviors that exemplify these factors). Without the behaviors, the impact is zero. People need to see something tangible before they believe in it – for example, actions and behaviors. Interest in something is never enough for leaders. Application from that interest has to result. For an analogy, think about love and a partner. It is usually not enough to tell them you love them, actions are required to prove the consistency in that statement.

Rapport and trust are paramount features in contemporary leadership. Alone, we may achieve a lot but with others committed to our goals, we can achieve at a higher level.

Rapport is the door to the building of trust (on a 1-2-1 basis), so we will consider this first.

Rapport skills

Rapport happens in the small-talk and spaces between the big talks. In other words we need to be engaged unhurriedly with people more often. For the greatest effect, these unhurried conversations happen when it is not strictly necessary to be talking at that moment. Creating such spaces makes an enormous statement:

> I am interested in you; at this moment you are more important than anything else on my agenda.

When we are busy chasing our own tail we rarely make time for such gestures, so prioritization and management of time are essential if these gestures are to be consistently applied. We shall see later that consistency in all the stages of building trust is essential, so it is best to keep our rapport skills in constant readiness at work, not just switched on (for effect) from time-to-time.

Here are some suggestions for consideration. What are the purposes of each action?

- Extend and develop contacts – especially those you know less well.

- Keep engaged in conversations and listen.

- Keep your cell-phone off in coffee breaks; stay with the group.

- Talk little.

- Show that you heard by reflecting back or asking a question.

- If someone expresses something of personal risk, acknowledge it and be prepared to express a brief experience of your own: 'It is probably not as interesting as your experience but I once . . .' honors their expression without stealing the show.

In each case we are putting people at the center of our action rather than as a requirement of acute need. If you only run to people when you need something, they will not respond well to you or go further than they have to. To consistently attend better to people, we probably need to revalue them in our priorities at work.

Beginnings, middles and ends

Whether we engage with people face-to-face, by phone or by e-mail there need to be three distinct parts to the process if people are to feel honored.

Beginnings

Favorites for face-to-face meetings remain:

Hi Tom, how's it going?

Hello Tom, how are you?

It's good to see you Tom. Did you have a good journey?

Each offers a question which makes its own oblique state-ment, 'I am interested in you'. Further, not one question jumps into a work context – each invites the person to share something personal rather than work-related. However, it does not prevent them from going to a work issue directly if they choose to do so. But the greeting and question are not enough. We must then actually leave a space for an answer and remain engaged with that person, not turning to greet someone else!

Here are similar beginnings for telephone use:

Oh Tom, it's good to hear from you. How are things with you?

Tom, how are you?

It's great to hear you Tom. How's life treating you?

Again, leave a space for a reply and if that reply is cursory (for example: 'fine and how are you?') be prepared to follow-up your question again to stimulate their contribution to the dance of rapport:

Things are really good, I'd heard you were abroad, how was that!

E-mails are like hornet's waiting to sting. In our desire to get to the point, to 'be professional' and save time, we often forget the necessity for politeness. In fact, because we have no idea of the circumstances in which the e-mail will be read, it is even more important to soften the introduction and demark each part of the communication process:

Tom, I hope things are good with you! I thought to drop a line to you now as I am preoccupied with. . . .

Tom, I know you are busy and hope things are going well for you! Could I ask you to help me with some information that I need pretty urgently. . . .

Tom, thanks for your mail. I understood you were away at the Paris conference. I hope things are fine! Did you contribute or find it useful! By the way, I'd like to ask . . .

Notice that the questions are often regarded as statements and the question-marks are often left out of the text. For example, 'I know you are busy and hope things are going well for you'. In the examples above we make our interest overt and use the mark in order to properly invite their engagement in the dance of rapport. I use the word 'dance' again, and advisedly so. Rapport-building involves a delicate process of give and take, as we shall see.

Middles

The middle cuts to the chase if you are initiating the contact for a reason. If you are responding, then the most important thing is to give your full consideration, whether it is an e-mail or a direct contact. The little extra effort, particularly with e-mail, is invariably noticed and welcome.

In your haste to get to the point the impact of a great beginning can be lost, as shown in this example of a face-to-face engagement:

> *Tom how are you I need you to get some information for the meeting tomorrow pretty much immediately and . . .*

Compare that with:

> *Tom* <pause> *How are you?* <pause and listen> *Listen, have you got a moment as I do need your help with something urgent.* <pause and look> *It's about tomorrow's meeting. I'm feeling exposed because I do not have the depreciation adjustments and my figures are not watertight. How quickly could you get those to me?*

The extra time involved is minimal but which do you think will have a better result and maintain or increase the rapport you have? The pauses are not just for effect. They also serve as cues to remind you that you need to be listening. If we just rush out a string of orders or statements, there is little time for noticing much about the (psychological) state of the person we are speaking to.

The pauses are also effectively used on the telephone. It gives both parties the chance to reflect a little and to listen.

The e-mail examples given above (see Beginnings) also show how to get to the middle. There are no pauses, but paragraphing serves the same purpose, by drawing a line under the polite entrée and getting swiftly to the main course.

Ends

Endings complete the process by honoring the time and attention that your recipient has given to you. Ignoring this can just cheapen the good effect made in the beginning. You can also usefully go slightly off topic to show interest in them. If they are contributing something helpful, think about expressing what that means to you in more personal terms than you might otherwise use. You might also mention their effort, attention and the time they are prepared to devote, and you can embellish all that whether face-to-face, phone or mail.

> *Tom, thanks for your time and commitment to this, I am grateful. It's great to have your support*

> *Tom, I have to go shortly, is there anything else you would like to add now?*

> *Tom, thanks for persisting through this stuff. If you could come back with those three sets of figures today I shall be very relieved indeed. I hope all goes well for you in San Antonio by the way.*

Notice the use of their name again. The fact that you use their name in the beginning and the end shows special effort on your part (especially if typed). With detailed e-mail, you may wish to consider summarizing the actions and expectations in a bulleted list format so that they are easy to notice.

Honoring and celebration

Honoring people is so important that it is referred to many times in this book. With so much emphasis on progress and success at work, the natural habit of thanking and honoring people is sometimes neglected. Each day that passes at work should provide us with at least one opportunity to thank or honor someone. We must be aware of people's efforts, especially when this goes beyond their contractual obligations. Some leaders have a natural tendency to thank and honor people; others need to do this systematically. If you are in the latter group then you might wish to set up a system of your own so that the extra efforts of all your people are regularly considered, and appropriate actions taken.

ACTIONS

With the constant pressure to perform and exceed targets we sometimes also forget the necessity to pause and mark our glory collectively. In Part One we saw that the Healthy Action Cycle needs an acknowledgment step following decision and action. Our people need this too. As leaders, rather than as managers, we will be looking for broader outcomes, including making it:

- Personal

- Welcome

- Involving

- Publicized at the higher levels.

E-mail is not nearly as personal, as a hand-signed letter sent to a home address. Face-to-face contact is always appreciated, especially if you are genuine in your appreciation and your expression is both generous and eloquent.

The method of marking or celebrating success needs to be a generally welcome affair. Time-consuming events or those that take people away from their families (and private) commitments, may not always be appreciated. An evening dinner may therefore not be welcomed by all, and a lunch or afternoon celebration in work-time may be more appropriate.

Collective celebration can work to build rapport and team spirit but is often spoiled by the lack of real feeling expressed by senior people. If you tend to be reserved, then consider a very brief introduction only. Do not wheel in more senior figures unless they are respected, popular and your staff feels comfortable and relaxed around them. Introduce someone who is excited and passionate about the outcome and is able to express the collective value of the team better than you can. This person could be two or more levels below you. Try to include people at all levels in the team in your notices and speeches, and the expression should be genuine and preferably have passion.

At celebrations, many managers cannot resist the desire to galvanize the troops for the next stage. This is not the moment for that, and this also applies to Christmas celebrations. Let the celebration stand on its own without reference to the future, as this only weakens the message of celebration. Some people will feel manipulated and deflated if you use these occasions to try to push them toward the next target. Honor them and encourage them to feel proud for creating what has been achieved. There will be time for galvanizing action tomorrow.

Provided the message is not overly sanitized (or ignores the contribution of key individuals to the success) then generation of PR internally (and beyond) can also be considered. If done well, this can help many in the team feel proud of their individual and collective achievements.

Mindsets for rapport and trust

A mindset is simply a collection of values, beliefs and a sense of self that help (or hinder) in a given situation. Clearly, it is useful to have some conscious control over our mental preparedness for situations. Obvious situations include mental preparation to speak at a conference or when dealing with an awkward stakeholder in the business. So let's consider mindsets appropriate for boosting effectiveness when employing rapport skills or building trust.

Here are some suggestions:

- I cannot run everything on my own.

- This business depends foremost on our people.

- People perform better when they feel regarded and trust their colleagues.

- My colleagues could trust me more if I give them more quality, 1-2-1 time.

- In times of crisis I need the best goodwill I can get.

- Taking time with people is important.

- To have more impact I need people who want to support me and my aims and in a team that has a multiplied effect.

- Most people are more interested in recognition than in rewards.

Do any immediate actions stem from consideration of these ideas? How will you know whether your actions have been effective and how will you assess or measure that effectiveness? What will you look for in terms of behaviors? How long might that take?

ACTIONS

MEASUREMENT

TIMESCALES

Trust

Trust takes time to develop but can be eroded or destroyed in an instant. Trust must be consistently applied in order to build it up. A serious slip can cause freefall and there is invari-

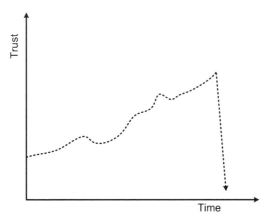

Figure 8.1 Trust building and freefall

ably a buffer-period when no recovery or improvement will be made (see Figure 8.1). This buffer-period may last hours, months and even years.

The curve in the diagram does not start at the bottom because people normally give you the benefit of the doubt until they get to know you. The level of that benefit varies enormously from person to person and from relationship to relationship. Freefall normally takes your standing below where it started! We shall return to the subject of trust and identify the seven trust factors in Chapter 10 (Leadership qualities).

Rapport and trust are helpful to the level of influence we can produce since the more people we can rely on, the wider our sphere of impact in the world. Many younger executives, including the author at an earlier stage, fight and scratch to get results at any cost. But real success comes when you have many people playing your game with you.

9

Relationship building: putting it together

W HEN WE WORK WITH PEOPLE THERE IS A GRADUAL development of interaction. This is the same in all relationships. I give a bit and you give a bit, and so on. Each individual relationship can be considered as a spread of cash investments to hedge against fluctuations in the market. In each area of investment you look for a return and if no return is forthcoming, you think about investing elsewhere.

These investments increase the level of holistic knowledge you have about one another. This increases rapport and trust, but may also increase respect.[1] For example, people often have skills or hobbies in their private lives that are extraordinary.

---

[1] One of the top employers in the USA is Analytical Graphics, Malvern, PA and they arrange fun events where people learn much more about the skills and talents of their coworkers. They report that this creates higher levels of mutual respect in their organization.

The areas that we can invest in for **each** person might include some or all of the following: private information, social interaction, exquisite listening, flexibility and doing favors. In each case, you might consider making at least two separate deposits of the same type before deciding to place your investment in another area.

Now, I would like you to think of someone influential in your work context (a peer in the business or someone outside your business) with whom you have a reasonable working relationship (over some time) but do not regard as a friend. Preferably this will be someone with whom you would like to have an improving relationship, but in fact there has been little change for some time.

In Table 9.1 there are two columns to be filled in from your perceptions of that relationship: one refers to what you do for them and the other refers to what they do for you. You might like to populate the grid with dots to indicate the frequency with which each factor has been invested by each of you, as shown.

Overall, you are looking for a balance of dots on both sides. It does not matter if the table is skewed – sometimes relationships do develop where investments are made in entirely different areas but function well.

If the table is unbalanced with many more dots on your side than the other, it may be worth considering some of the other factors (approaches) in which you have not invested. These actions may or may not bring a response; some people are

Table 9.1 Co-worker relationships

Factor	What I do for them	What they do for me
Example	• • • • •	• • •
Offer accommodation (favor)		
Offer compromise (give and take)		
Offering collaboration (co-work)		
Exquisite attention in social interaction		
Accessible in times of need		
Help/support in times of need		
Shared facts about private life		
Shared sensitive, personal information, weaknesses, etc.		
Shared personal belief or value		

takers! However, two fresh investments in one factor area will be enough to see if there is a reciprocated effort.

If there are more dots on the right hand column, it may be worth thinking about reciprocating more. This may involve doing more of what you already do, but a greater impact (whether favorable or not) will be had by doing something differently. This is particularly true if nothing is changing – in which event doing something different is the only sure way of making a difference.

If you have many dots in your area and none on the other, consider whether in fact these types of events are welcome to the co-workers. Could you have a conversation with them to discuss that and invite feedback?

ACTIONS

10

Leadership qualities

Traits, trust factors and people skills

Let's look at typical leadership qualities and see how these might help us to develop actions that will make a difference in the way we work. These same actions may help others to want to follow us.

In our training courses, delegates are often asked to come up with the key qualities of people that have inspired them as leaders. Although sometimes contradictory, many of the same traits appear again and again. The items in Table 10.1 give a summary of many such lists. The abbreviation TF stands for 'trust factor'. The table lists 11 leadership qualities: seven leader traits and four people skills. One of the leader traits, Credible, has at least eight factors.

Table 10.1   Traits, trust factors and people skills

Leadership qualities	Notes
Leader traits	
Clear communicator – the big picture, the details, the boundaries and desired behaviors	
Straight-talker	
Flexible	
Reliable and consistent (TF)	
Accepts responsibility (TF)	Takes the can
Discrete (TF)	Safe with information
Credible	See list of eight
Knowledgable	In specifics
Willing to be decisive when urgent action is needed	
Crystallizer: can pin-point critical factors in complex situations	
Can be charismatic	Not essential
Has – and communicates – vision	
Takes (measured) risks	Considered actions
Walks the talk (TF)	Does as preaches
Authentic (TF)	Is the real thing
People skills	
Listens intently	Can reflect speech
Understands motivations	Flexible approach
Supportive of me (TF)	Encouraging
Interested in me (TF)	Remembers details

Trust factors

Among the leadership qualities there are seven key trust factors that appear to be most common in leaders, five from personal leader traits and two that are people skills. Errors made in these seven key trust areas can impact badly on individuals but worse, have a broad, detrimental effect on the team. It can take a long time to get back the confidence of people as a result, as we saw in the earlier scenario of 'freefall'. This then tends to demark the difference between trust factors and the other leadership qualities. There is room for an occasional lapse in the other qualities and it may not be noticed. A leader must exhibit consistently high behaviors in ALL SEVEN trust factors to succeed. Failure to maintain consistent behaviors in any trust factor can be very damaging. Here are the seven trust factors listed:

- Reliable and consistent

- Accepts responsibility

- Discrete

- Walks the talk

- Authentic

- (Demonstrably) supportive of people

- (Demonstrably) interested in people

Let's look briefly at all the leadership qualities in turn with special attention to each trust factor. I am not just trying to bring life to the model but am looking for real applications that could impact on what you actually do.

> *A leader must exhibit consistently high behaviors in ALL SEVEN trust factors to succeed*

Trait: Clear communicator

Clear communication involves abilities greater than just being able to make clear overviews or get into the fine detail where necessary. Clear communication also requires the skill of understanding one's audience and tailoring the communication for the greatest impact.

Remember that people are stimulated differently by the same language. And most people prefer to have information visually presented rather than in tables or text. In practice, when communicating with groups we have to embrace a number of media and language options to stimulate different people. For more information about communication styles, see McLeod (2006).

Boundaries and desired behaviors

Clear communication also requires that people know how they are expected to behave and so explicit communication of the expectations are important. We also need to be sure that these expectations are reasonably aligned to those within the organization as a whole.

Expectations for behavior operate in every sphere of human relationship from rearing children and obeying the law, to the corporate world. There is comfort and 'security' in knowing what the limits are, especially if there are serious consequences for going over those limits.

I mention boundaries and 'desired behaviors' in the same breath, because there are two approaches. One is to tell people what they must not do (state the limits); the other is to tell them what they are expected to do (state behavioral expectations). On balance, I believe that a combination of both works best in most organizations but, in practice, unfortunately, most rely on statements of boundaries only. The problem of that is that when you set up boundaries, there is a good chance that some people will see it as a challenge to break that boundary, just 'because it is there and stated in the negative'. Analytical Graphics is an exception among businesses. They have a mantra that runs, 'Do the right thing and we do not need to have rules' (boundaries). Instead it has a policy book that describes what people are expected to do, the 'desired behaviors'. Of course that policy book is a corporate document, not divisional or departmental. At the sub-corporate level the behavioral requirements are not so explicit. Analytical Graphics hire people who are flexible and take initiative in all aspects of their work, including noticing the rules that are tacit rather than stated clearly. They tend to hire people who need both the security of procedures and explicit boundaries, for obvious reasons.

The desired behaviors within an organization will be numerous and many will be specific to functional areas – for example, client-contact recording, pricing information disclosure, and so on. Managers may have expectations about honesty, meeting targets on time, communication with appropriate stakeholders and many other issues. Strong personalities sometimes set personal expectations that do not match the corporate ones. An example might be someone who is inflexible about time-keeping even though the corporation generally permits some give-and-take for those staff who put extra effort and time into their work. Their expectations might be respected but resented. However, if there is a direct or indirect benefit for your people due to your variant expectation, then it may be appreciated. An example might be allowing payroll staff to leave three hours early on a Thursday because they are regularly working late into the evening on a Tuesday to complete the weekly payroll.

If we fail to provide expectation of what is acceptable in clear terms, then people inadvertently or deliberately overstep the boundaries. This underlines the advantage of providing clarity in both the boundaries and the desired behaviors.

When setting boundaries, there has to be a dynamic balance between the need for control and the need for achievement. It is a fact that in many large organizations the achievement of things on time involves the reworking of desired behaviors (exceeding authority) in order to succeed. We need boundaries and clear expectations of behavior in order to improve efficiency and to maintain financial controls, consistency and quality.

These same requirements can sometimes prevent achievement when they become overburdensome or when there are so many controls that the process of doing anything is limited. Imagine an order for one of your products that will be delivered on a phantom basis. You will not supply it but complete all the paper, computer entries and sign-off procedures to achieve its delivery on time. How long does that take? Imagine this same process with a development process producing a new product, and you see that with no productive work, the process itself consumes weeks or months of time. Since it is overhead, it makes sense to reduce it while maintaining sufficient controls to satisfy corporate and customer needs.

Expectations overstepped

The limits of boundaries need to be overt, and different leaders will have different ways of dealing with people who have gone too far. An analogous situation is that of failure. Generally we should welcome failure as an opportunity for learning and we should be embarrassed if the same failure happens twice. 'Failure, Forward, Fast' is the mantra of Gavin Newsom,[1] it represents a positive philosophy for learning from failure and is also applicable here. We want the individual or group to understand the issue and learn from it. Others may need to learn too. Restating the boundaries is not enough, we need also to state the expectations we have for the desired behaviors. We need to move forward quickly.

In a serious situation of negligence or deliberate sabotage, another level of response will be required. At what point are people exceeding their authority for the greater good (whether successful or not) and at what point are they undermining your trust, putting the organization in jeopardy or being a poor role-model for other team-members? The answers to these

---

[1] Once Mayor of San Francisco.

questions have to be personal to you and governed by both corporate and personal values. As you can see from the above, these two should ideally be closely aligned. At no point will a leader just let errant behavior pass on the basis that 'it may not happen again'. Leadership demands self-reflection and decision-making. If there is an action, then what you have to say needs to be clear and unambiguous. Typically you will wish to deal with the person or people involved.[2] Sometimes the issue is very important and there is a risk that it may be repeated. In this event the learning has to be broadcast more widely. Each situation will require a specific-context response.

Trait: Straight-talker

Sometimes it is necessary to tell it how it is. The bigger the organization below us, and the greater the complexity of the reporting system, the greater the potential for people to interpret and develop sub-messages that are detrimental to the team. In the West we tend to err on the side of caution and, as a result, misunderstandings and loss of productivity are common. If the news is unwelcome or a shock, it may be necessary to communicate it more than once, taking care to make sure that the potential for misinterpretation is minimal by using the same language, same phrases and key messages as before.

---

[2] Please see 'facilitating the 1-2-1' for descriptions of how to provide feedback in ways that are heard, understood and, further, provide the individuals with specific expectations about their future behaviors (what you want to notice them doing, rather than what you don't!).

Trait: Flexible

I generally want to know that my bosses care about my needs and that they will adapt to suit those needs. People who work for us generally want these things also.

Any amount of exquisite listening to people will make no difference if we remain permanently resolute and unbending. This does not mean falling over. People have an impression of the norm of anyone's behavior, and will recognize instantly when they feel favored. You can be very hard-line in your approach to business but still be able to favor people with tiny adaptations and favors for their benefit. Even small tokens can be as impactful as the large gestures made by others who are much more flexible. It's the variation from the norm (wherever that is pitched) that makes the difference.

We introduced the concept of boundaries and desired behaviors in the 'Clear communicator' section above. Boundaries are partly overt (rules and limits) and desired behaviors can be overt by publishing them. The expectations of behavior arise from both boundaries and desired behaviors. We also provide an example by our what-we-do-here consistency and by our behaviors (including reactions) toward our people generally.

As leaders, when we use our flexibility to favor someone, a quick mental check is necessary to question the impact for the individual concerned (new boundary?) and the broader implications for others who will know, or may find out, what you have agreed.

Flexibility can work for us or against us. It supports us when flexible solutions are favorable to individuals or teams. It works against us when people interpret flexibility as favoring other people (or groups) and when people misinterpret flexible behavior as shifty (or moving values on a whim). Flexibility is essential in modern leadership because the demands (and culturally accepted rights) of people have transformed so remarkably over the last few decades. Additionally, the pressures of the global-village demand faster decisions. A leader thus needs to be consciously flexible and aware of the potential for misinterpretation.

Years ago, my partner wrote off her car. The FD of my company loaned me a second company vehicle for as long as would be necessary to test drive and buy a replacement. This was done on the explicit proviso that this gesture would remain invisible to everyone in the business. It did not cost the company very much as the car was on a term-lease arrangement with a fixed value. The gesture built-in a higher level of rapport (collusion if you will) that I hope was paid off measurably by my effort and loyalty to the FD and the business for much longer than the actual loan of the vehicle.

Where patterns of circumstance demand flexible solutions, so flexible patterns of response are also needed. These new flexible patterns of behavior eventually become 'what are predictable, reliable and consistent'. But that takes time, because people need exposure to experience and learn that the boundaries are routinely different in different circumstances. For example, you may be an inclusive and reasonable collaborator with unions when considering new reward and recognition structures within your organization, but you may also be very firm with them when it comes to the issue of reducing the numbers and locations of manufacturing plants for long-term cost savings (due to your knowledge of trends in manufacturing costs). There is flexibility, but that flexibility is consistently applied in given contexts.

Flexible boundaries that have no logic to them are a destabilizing issue. Nobody really knows where they stand or how far they can push. Some will push further than you expect, and waste your time. Flexible boundaries that follow logical processes (in each context) may be challenging but not destabilizing.

- Do your people know where their boundaries are?

- Do some of them overstep the mark with negative consequences?

- What needs to be communicated to change that?

- What would motivate them to change their behaviors individually?

- If they overstep with positive consequences ought the boundaries to be shifted?

ACTIONS

Trait: Reliable and consistent (TF)

In groups the word 'reliability' has links with the word 'consistent'. And these descriptors seem, on the surface, to work contrary to the need to be flexible. The discussion above has, I hope, also brought you to consider that reliability and consistency are also context-specific. People's need for reliability and consistency depends upon the context, but will be experienced as sets of behaviors that can be logically explained and are predictable **in each context**. In other words, reliable 'in that context'. An example might be an immediate need for rapid decision-making as opposed to a style of leadership that is more involving in the day-to-day operations. A reliable leader will behave in predictable ways in each context even though the behaviors are very different. To that extent the behaviors can also be rationalized simply – there is comfort and 'security' in that – people know what to expect. Consistency is also necessary in the behaviors that are exhibited by the trust factors. As we see above, consistent behaviors keep the ship in calm seas. One lapse creates a ripple that can create a long-term wave of discomfort.

We are reliable when people depend upon us. If we set up an expectation and fail to satisfy that, then people will be disappointed or hurt. Failing several times will destroy loyalty and, as a result, performance may reduce, particularly if you need something from them that is of no benefit to them but of value to you.

The real problem for leaders is not just an acknowledgment that other people are more or less sensitive to such lapses; it is knowing specifically what those sensitivities are for each and every person. In the following list, set down your own sensitivities for the actions described as if they had just this minute happened to you for the second time. Provide a rating from 0 to 10 where the most negative impact on you is 10.

Event: My boss . . .	Rating
• postponed my annual 1-2-1 on the day	......
• changed his mind about my attending an important meeting or event	......
• failed to put a target department under my command while restructuring	......
• introduced some colleagues (but not me) to a dignitary	......
• did not give much emphasis to my achievements in the annual report	......
• failed to turn up to open my divisional conference	......
• backed away from a disciplinary procedure adversely affecting me	......
• took credit for a project that I led	......
• froze a budget necessary to achieve target	......
• froze hiring the talent necessary to achieve target	......

Your profile is almost unique. The people who work for you will all have different ones. Clearly, if we fail to make a commitment or meet an expectation then we need a strategy for dealing with that. A simple three-step process will help to ameliorate the damage done:

1. Firstly, say sorry and mean it. This should preferably be done face-to-face.

2. Secondly, warmly seek feedback from them about their reaction and feelings (if they will share those with you).

3. Thirdly, reflect what you have heard, and if you make any promises then keep them unfailingly.

This process will not necessarily save face but may help you to redeem yourself. There are only so many times that people will accept this and, again, everyone is different. How tolerant are you? How many times would you accept such treatment before you took action to escape the situation completely?

Trait: Accepts responsibility (TF)

A key trust factor, the acceptance of responsibility is a paramount quality in leaders. When things go wrong, people need to know that the manager is taking the initiative and supporting the team. Also, that if push comes to shove, the responsibility will stop with the manager rather than be passed down. One false move can poison a little-valued staff-member and that can poison goodwill and have long-term repercussions in the entire team.

Dick was a Financial VP. His company required restructuring for a substantial investment of cash. His team went through about 15 separate negotiations over three years. They all failed, which was largely due to his inflexibility. He was not capable in the area of compromise, which was a serious issue. Hit-rates in such cases do vary widely but the chances were weakened by using a poor choice of negotiator. He never admitted his failings but was happy to pitch blame in every other direction. The impact was entirely negative. The involvement of team-members in the support of negotiations became unenthusiastic and matter-of-fact. Morale worsened.

Jeremy was COO of a manufacturing operation in Europe that had a history of over 70 years of development and production. The business was owned by a major group and it was obvious that, within five years at most, the company would need to manufacture overseas. The group was reluctant to damage a historical operation. After a number of business proposals and meetings over several months the decision was made to close the factory totally within a period of eight months, with manufacturing going to China. Jeremy had kept the entire workforce up to date, always being upbeat but not evading the fact that the whole business depended upon every person meeting quality and production targets. It was the stature of the man that he carried his people with him to the brink and beyond. He informed everyone himself and tirelessly worked to assist and help the staff to find new jobs. I have no doubt at all that if he calls on any one of his staff to work for him again, they will follow him.

When you do take the blame, make sure that all the team-members know what you have done. Brief your people accordingly:

I have had a very difficult meeting with the Board and explained that I have been unable to bring the Strident Project to fruition as funding is still four million short. They have decided to pull the project. This should not reflect on Tim who has worked tirelessly under my direction. We have learned lessons from the experience but I have to say that, even with hindsight, I do not believe we could have done more to get Strident off the ground. I have taken full responsibility for the lack of success. It is a measure of my belief in Tim that he is to lead the new Probus Project starting the first of next month. We will take the learning forward and with your help and support both agree that Probus will be a success story.

Trait: Discrete (TF)

Discretion is also a key trust factor. People learn, over some time, that the confidential information they share should not be leaked. Lapses can lead to a sudden and widespread loss of trust. We are privy to much information. It is not clever to express confidential material in any circumstance – it is destructive and eventually the mud will stick. Frankly, if you lack discretion you are not yet a leader. You will fail to influence your people or have them follow you if you are not regarded as a safe-repository for confidential information.

Trait: Credible

We have identified eight of the key factors that support credibility. They are summarized individually below.

Knowledgable

It is typically the case that most leaders are not superbly competent at all the jobs done by the people that report to them – there are exceptions, particularly where the role is a recent promotion within the same business area. However, the leader must be able to understand and communicate his or her understanding of the critical factors at a reasonably detailed level of language. This is a challenge in new roles. A priority in a new job must be taking time to research each area well. This conflicts with our desire to make a difference. Research well and bide your time. People expect you to make reasoned changes – not ill-considered actions that lack holistic soundness. Short-cutting the research is ill-advised. Adjustments that are properly considered with an open mind, free from rapid judgment and open to persuasive argument by others will save you time later. However, a thorough knowledge provides a safety-net when short-term problems need to be addressed decisively. Without adequate research and understanding, any rapid response will have unseen implications that may prove very detrimental to the business and to you.

Our knowledge should not be fixed. The details change with time and leaders must make time to keep up-to-date and stay fresh. Apart from reading and questioning, some of the most useful knowledge comes from informal conversations with colleagues who trust you. They can then open up and be honest with their feedback, sharing doubts as well as certainties because they know that you are discrete, measured and fair. It is good practice to ask direct questions if you have the necessary rapport:

> *Tom, I hear your confidence but also would like to be updated on every doubt, however small, so that I am prewarned and might have some input in helping you to repair anything that needs to be perfected before we go live with the new network.*

If all we hear is positives we are working in the dark. We must know the weaknesses, the doubts and the fears and help our people to work their way into success. Leaders who become too big to listen fall fastest.

Willing to be decisive when urgent action is needed

As we know, there are times to lead and times to manage. Vacillation is seen comprehensively as a weakness in the same way that poor decision-making is viewed. Successful decisions come from good research and excellent knowledge tempered by experience, not the other way around. If these three factors are in good order, then in acute situations a rapid decision should be feasible.

- What acute situations have arisen or could arise in your work?

- Do you know enough detail to make the best possible decisions?

- How can you ameliorate that/or improve your own research and knowledge?

ACTIONS

If self-confidence is a factor that is holding you back (rather than ignorance of the facts and the implications) then it is time to consider setting up peer-discussions and/or coaching at the earliest opportunity.

Crystallizer: Can pin-point critical factors in complex situations

Leaders need to allow creative answers to arise from complex situations. Ultimately, however, there is a point when facilitation needs to be stopped and a focused debate or decision made. Typically, the need to slow the creative process and focus is forced by time issues – for example, in technical team meetings where immediate progress is essential, but where people have flown in and will otherwise have infrequent opportunities to meet again.

A leader will gauge the need to focus but not necessarily act immediately. Other considerations may be important and so questions may first need to be answered by colleagues.

Can be charismatic

I am often asked whether one can learn to be charismatic. I suspect that a few people develop these qualities early, but the rest of us develop aspects of charisma through self-development. Charismatic people have the advantage of 'branding' – a collection of value-judgments about them that becomes culturally accepted folklore. For those who develop similar traits (usually slowly) it is too late to create such branding. An exception can occur where a leader is brought into a new business that is remote from their previous organization. Their traits may be the same in both jobs but the baggage of cultural perception is left behind and so a new 'brand' can be created around them. This is worth considering in your own career progression.

- How many new ideas can you test and apply now to find out which are most successful for you?

- How many of these new strategies might you be able to launch in a fresh job or another organization?

ACTIONS

Has – and communicates – vision

The whole area of vision is so obvious that I will not dwell on it too long. There are many stories of how the individual or group vision creates radically inspiring results and a number of excellent texts to provide information on how to set up the visioning processes in the index. In *Performance Coaching* (Mcleod, 2003) I cite the example of Christo, the object artist whose ability to galvanize different groups of people to wrap up buildings and islands in fabric is widely known. Against the highest possible odds, he repeatedly succeeds in projects that have no obvious, intrinsic value to many of those involved in them. In that way they are even more exceptional than obvious cases of visionary objectives where the participants all gain something tangible.

In creating visions, most of us need to rely heavily on research-ing and (preferably) involving our people to develop the vision so that the buy-in factor is carefully developed. Leaders of organizations need buy-in and involvement at all levels. To get that they develop processes of involvement by generating and communicating empowered visions that offer tangible strategies for challenge, contribution and success. Where people feel that they are being challenged, that they can make a valuable contribution, and that they can develop trust in the success of the whole project, then one has a movement – a tide of energy – that is irresistible.

'Great leaders' who led from the front by dictating and order-ing alone may have had more failures than successes. We keep more options open if we can listen and harness our troops.

It is common to bring groups together to develop vision, but so often this is left to a subset of the main operating Board. Ideally, vision, is created more widely by extending the man-agement committee or Board and bringing a wider range of stakeholders into the process. Goals will arise from visioning processes and if we want powerful motivation then we need to involve more of the people who will be instrumental in creating that situation. Goals are not often produced by the most senior people in the business. We do better to involve more of the people who impact and understand our objectives from all aspects. In all cases we need probing questions to go beyond what is developmental and evolving from trends. Trends give us confidence about the next period of economic activity, but do not create new visions and goals that propel us into a new league. Questions like these do that:

- If we knew for sure that there would be no organic growth for the next five years, how could we produce increased revenues and margins?

- What do we really supply our clients?

- If we are not really suppliers of commercial reports but suppliers of confidence, reliability and speed, what else could we do to satisfy these other needs?

ACTIONS

Takes (measured) risks

Not all people rate the taking of risks as a leadership quality, but it invariably features on group lists. A level of challenge and any success that follows does help to create a 'can-do' confidence in organizations, and hence the notion that calculated risk has a potential cultural gift to bring to the team. This is especially the case in an organization that was tainted by failure, by a series of acquisitions or by sequential restructurings and has been diminished by those experiences. Changing to a 'can-do' philosophy, backed up by systems and resources, can solve that.

A culture of measured risk can also arise from within an organization where a clear and attractive vision is created by its leaders. As a result, if done well, there is eagerness to develop that vision, provided it also creates a future that brings security, confidence and where people feel that they play a significant part.

The formula of risk and success is one that inspires confidence, and that is the key spin-off for a leader. Clearly the organization must be amenable to coping with risk–success and risk–failure. Where an organization is inexperienced in risk-taking, a new leader may need to develop confidence by taking risks that are measured to suit the culture. The new leader can then build the level of risk (within his or her own competences) with time in order to carry the same, confident, people.

Cultural factors are more important when it comes to failure and the reactions to that. If one is unsure, then a useful strategy is to consider and discuss the potential for failure and the implications of it with all stakeholders so that they are aware of that possibility, and know that there is a strategy in place for that too.

Walks the talk (TF)

Some organizations are led by people who expect a different set of behaviors (from others) than they are willing to exemplify themselves. There are exceptions – for example, McDonald's food chain, where management at all levels is culturally expected to serve at the retail-counters and gain from regular exposure to their customers. 'Walking the talk' is a trust factor and so, again, we need to demonstrate absolute consistency.

We quite rightly pour scorn on politicians who talk about environmental concerns but travel in limousines and helicopters, and those who talk about the value of family and are caught out having affairs. The errors that we make may not be as monumental but the grapevine is just as effective and can undermine the impact we have with our team. It is also true, in larger organizations, that the image of the most senior people can be tarnished by innuendo and untruths.

Walking the talk is another factor that builds confidence in those around you and to that extent it is very like reliability and consistency. If you are not willing to walk your own talk then you are best to keep quiet and let someone else walk it for you.

To be known as someone who 'walks the talk' at all levels, we need to be accessible and seen by people at those levels. Eating in private dining rooms far from our canteens, having separate buildings and car-parks and private suites where only the powerful are allowed to tread, are things that keep our image open to manipulation. To a lesser extent, managers lower down the organization can also suffer from the same process of diminishing impact if they do not understand the necessity to be seen and accessible at all levels.

Let's assume that you are cost-cutting in your area. What cuts will you openly make in your own offices? Let's imagine that you have tasked all your people to bring more added-value to their activities. What added value will you bring and how will you make that obvious?

These arguments may seem facile but they carry great impact in effect. Asking others to go through arduous processes without attending to the same criteria yourself is not a way to win adherence and loyalty. Walking the talk is.

ACTIONS

Authentic (TF)

Authenticity forms the basis for Chapter 19 (The Real Thing at Work) in Part Three, and we will go much more deeply into this subject than appropriate to this list. Here it is appropriate to highlight that authenticity is the opposite of playing the role. It is bringing the best of self into the role in a thoughtful way and with integrity, honesty and absolute believability. These factors are impactful, attractive and inspire the greatest possible loyalty.

People skills

I have isolated key people skills from what I call leader traits because the people skills represent the vehicle for engaging motivated work and disseminating our impact with massive effect. This starts in the key group of influencers to whom we have most access. By influencing them, we can augment the impact of culture-change significantly. These influences ought quite rightly to be addressed thoughtfully on a 360-degree basis; to our bosses, key stakeholders, our peers, those who work for us and those who work for others but are important or influential in other areas of the business. Leaders thoughtfully plan how to influence at strategic and tactical levels.

- Who are the key individuals on whom your influencing skills need to be focused to have the greatest possible impact?

- Do you have a systematic plan for developing that influence with each person?

- What is their preferred method of communication?

- How, when and where are you best placed to influence each of them?

ACTIONS

People skill: Listens intently

There are two qualities that distinguish the modern leader from those of old. They are: the proportion of time they spend listening, and the quality of that listening. Leaders no longer believe they have all the best answers or know the best way of motivating all their people, all of the time. Instead, they rely on information, thoughtful mental processing and feedback.

Exquisite listening skills are not only important for our own learning but also to have impact. Necessarily, if you have listened well and are flexible as managers, actions should flow from these conversations so that people know that they have the power to influence you also. They then feel part of your management rather than being subjected to it, and may feel that the relationship is special. It is a fact that people generally wish to feel special and differentially treated. Exquisite listening skills are a great way to encourage all those around us to feel like that! It's a paradox but one worth developing.

So what are exquisite listening skills? There are a number of behaviors that contribute to this, some of which are listed below.

Eye contact

Listening in 1-2-1 contact will involve eye contact. The use of eye contact should be comfortable for each of you. If you are in the habit of not looking at people, especially in the first moments of your communication, then you are disadvantaged. The information you need to gauge your impact is in front of you.

When listening, exaggerated leaning and staring can be off-putting. Make your eye contact graceful and easy. If the person starts to talk about something that you interpret as emotionally loaded, be mindful that the limits of their emotional intelligence may be higher than yours and maintain a relaxed manner and maintain the same, comfortable level of eye contact.

Some years ago, I met with the global HR VP of a major petroleum company. His suite and personal office were enormous and while I walked across to his desk he did not look up. He presented his hand without looking up. I was with him for almost a full hour and he only made eye contact fleetingly, for less than a second, as he rose to shake my hand. He walked me out to the outer office but made no eye contact as he bid me goodbye. I did not enjoy the experience one bit and did not want to work for him.

Listening without interruption

If you need to ask a question for clarity, then of course do so but for the most part listening well is best. If you feel a need to record some notes or are losing track you might say, at an appropriate pause:

> *Tom, I think I am hearing you right but would like to summarize what you said to be sure I have understood correctly. If it's okay with you I would like to take some notes as well. Is that okay?*

Summarizing gives you a chance to exhibit that you have really heard well. This is especially important where the issue being expressed is one that has been mentioned repeatedly. When that happens you can be sure that the person does not feel that you have heard properly (whether you did or not understand well). After summarizing invite the person to correct your understanding.

Judgment-free, open and alert

While we make judgments we are not truly listening. When listening we may do other mental processes that shut down our listening skills. These include:

- Interpreting

- Comparing

- Anticipating

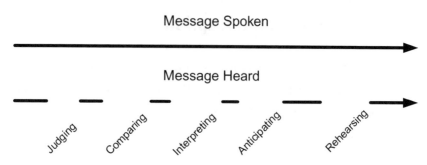

Figure 10.1 Missing the message due to thinking instead of listening

- Judging

- Rehearsing.

If we are to listen well then we need to be able to listen without a lot of mental processing. Otherwise we may be hearing, but not taking in key elements of the message. At the same time we will miss other body language and miss any mismatch between what is being said and what the speaker's body language may be demonstrating.

Hot-words

We all choose our words deliberately. We have thousands of possibilities to choose how we arrange those words but each individual selects their own special form. In most cases, people have particular sensitivities to particular words that they use and these are called 'hot-words'.

A hot-word could be any of the following, but the single characteristic of them all is that they probably carry emotive power. As such, they need to be noticed and care taken in referring back to them in the conversation. The hot-words might include:

- Any value-judgment referring to themselves

- Action words about self, like accomplished, managed, developed

- A named emotion

- Sensory words, like 'felt' and 'sensed'

- Expletives

- Words that sound out of place

- Precision words

- Extreme value-judgments (both positive and negative) about others.

We will look each of these in more detail shortly.

When an individual uses 'hot-words' it can be very useful to reuse those words rather than reinterpret them. If you do reinterpret, they will assume that you are not listening, or worse, that you may be undervaluing them or falsely exaggerating their positives for effect. There are exceptions, and these are explained below.

Value-judgments about self

A value-judgment about self is likely to be a hot-word. Imagine that you have just told your boss that you consider yourself particularly expert at X. Later in the conversation you hear him refer to your expertise as 'quite good'. If this does not make you bristle, come up with another 'positive' word that would annoy you – pretty good, reasonably good, not-bad-at, and competent? By now you should fully understand the dangers in the reinterpretation of hot-words!

Action words about self

These follow exactly the pattern of value-judgments about self. If someone chooses to use the phrase,

I directed the program personally

a non-reflective reference to that by you will probably upset them! For example,

Of course you had some involvement in that program didn't you?

It is best to reuse their word. If you object, then just leave out the verb completely:

With your intimate knowledge of the program could you offer some thoughts about . . .

Similar action words that may be 'hot' will include:

- Achieved

- Created

- Succeeded

- Co-worked

- Motivated

- Developed

- Managed

- Led

- Championed

- Partnered

- Thought-led.

Any set of people when asked to place these words in a list, with the most impressive first, will get different results. Semantics are important.

Named emotions

Emotional expression may include the naming of specific emotions. These are likely to have very specific and individual meanings for a given person in a given situation. Alter these at your peril! Here are some examples of non-reflective dialogue:

Tom: *I was devastated by the results.*
NFD: *That must have been traumatic for you.*

Tom: *I consider that a less than perfect outcome.*
NFD: *So tell me more about this failure.*

Tom: *I am upset by what she said in the open forum.*
NFD: *What was it she said to unbalance you like that?*

For some people any of these answers might work; for others their interpretation of this new word in the conversation is likely to be met with annoyance and a tangential and unproductive dialogue.

The word 'traumatic' has a direct association with the verb 'traumatized' which some will find more of a weakness than being 'devastated', and vice versa of course.

Similarly, the word 'unbalanced' may suggest mental aberrations. The word 'considering' is not an emotion but is probably a signal that the individual has semantic[3] attachment with the word because their EQ is low.

The use of the word 'failure' instead of 'upset' may seem overly aggressive and judgmental. If you felt strongly that the

---

[3] Semantics is the study of the meaning of language.

phrase, 'less than perfect outcome' was understated then you might ask:

> *Tom, you say that the outcome was less than perfect and I have to agree with you. But, could you summarize the affects in detail for me?*

A question like this will encourage individuals to start processing information. If they were fooling themselves, they will soon have a more productive sense of reality.

Sensory words

There are analogous situations involving sensory words to those where emotion is expressed. Sensory words describe how a person received information and many people have a very personal interpretation for these words and may reject any other descriptor at all. Beware of interpreting them and beware also of introducing a sensory word that they have not used:

Tom: *I was frankly disappointed by Irene's lack of professionalism.*
NRD: *I understand that you felt disappointed.*
Tom: *What have feelings to do with it?*

Tom: *In my estimation she wished to control the activities of the division any way she could.*
NRD: *What made you interpret Irene that way?*
Tom: *I did not interpret at all, I was aware of specifics.*

Tom: *I saw exactly what she did.*
NRD: *You think she made a sign with her finger?*
Tom: *No. I saw exactly that she made that sign.*

In this last case the sensory word is 'saw' but the word 'exactly' is also a hot word. When you have two or more hot words in a sentence, be sure to get them all right as the situation is likely to be highly charged for that individual.

Expletives

It is a matter of professional and personal etiquette whether you reflect expletives. However, the same rules apply – do not change the word for another, instead, replace the word using 'that' as in:

Tom, when she said that, do you think anyone else heard her?

Beware of patronizing,

Tom, I hear that you feel strongly

since the response may be,

I don't feel strongly. I am completely livid by what has been done to me!

Sometimes there may be a case for adjourning a meeting and letting the steam run out.

Tom, excuse me a minute but I need to take a comfort break, sorry. I shall not be very long. May I get you a coffee while I am out of the office?

The question helps Tom to process something else and deflects his attention for a moment. The pause, with luck, will enable him to reflect, let the heat out and produce a more productive situation when you return.

Words sounding out-of-place

We are not speaking of words used incorrectly out of ignorance. Even then, reflecting the word as they use it is probably better than correcting them pointedly. It is better to avoid the word. Hot words may be hot simply because of the history of the individuals or because the word is used in their cultural set. They may be more or less sensitized to them. If you do not know, the safe bet is to reuse that word. You will notice these words because they seem odd. Reflect them unless the word creates in them a particularly unhelpful mental state. The clue to that will be their state when they use the word, particularly if it is stressed, spat out, or if they are agitated.

If you are uncomfortable dealing with such situations then avoid reuse of the word or phrase that is used. Instead, say something like:

> *Tom, I believe I have heard you correctly. What might I do to help you in this situation do you think?*

Precision words

Words of measurement, whether about their own work or the work of others, may be hot and are best reflected back.

Tom: *I should say the productive impact was rather small*

NRD: *So this little benefit represents what to the bottom-line?*

The above non-reflective reply is likely to get a poor response. If you wish to make a point it could usefully be posed as a question as that may allow your listener to arrive at your interpretation without feeling judged by you.

Tom: *I think my report was valuable*

Angus: *Okay, I'm interested in that. In what ways is your report valuable?*

If they hedge, just summarize anything useful that they said (in answer to the question) and repeat the question in this way:

Angus: *Thanks Tom, I hear that Phil appreciated getting the report on time. Good, but in what other ways is your report valuable?*

This is the method of broken-record technique.[4] It is politely very forceful since it leaves no escape route. If you change the language you end up with a debate about the semantics of that language. Stay with the same phrasing that they were stuck with and they will process some more in order to get some fresh perspective. To do that they may need some silent processing space. Hold that silence and wait for the result.

---

[4] The broken-record technique prevents the artful thinker from dodging the question or statement. It is important not to use it aggressively since we want the person to think, pause and self-realize. If you are aggressive the thinker will not pause, he will react! See, for example, McLeod (2006).

Extreme value-judgments about others

As with expletives, these may be best referred to using the word 'that'. It is helpful for people to have somewhere to vent their anger. Ideally you will be comfortable about being used for that purpose if it is a private conversation that cannot be heard by others. If so, you then have the chance of helping them to reinterpret their experience more positively. If that is not within your current skills, it may again be appropriate to create a natural break.

A helpful aim, once the emotions have subsided, is to ask questions that help them to get greater perspective and come to a more useful and positive state from which to take useful actions (to improve the quality of their relating).

> *Tom, if they had another motive, what might that other motive be?*

> *Tom, why do you think this matter is so important to them?*

These questions invite new perspectives, and if a person is frustrated and stuck, new perspectives will develop choices and potential actions for changing the situation.

Summarize using reflective language[5]

We introduced the idea of repeating words when considering the approach to 'hot words'. This is called 'reflective language'

---

[5] For more detailed description and examples, refer to McLeod (2003).

and involves using those same words and phrases precisely. What is the point of that? The brain is largely geared to noticing differences to the norm. When we say a phrase, a neural pathway in the brain opens up which is like the lock in a door; the key is the phrase. When that same phrase is used in the same way, this key re-enters the lock easily without initiating logical, interpretive processing. When you listen well, you can reflect the words and phrases you hear in your responses.

Reflective language helps individuals to feel heard. More than that, they can stay more perfectly in their own stories without having to negotiate with you about the world in your head. In fact, many of the most popular (and best listeners) that we know do this automatically, without thinking. These skills are easily learned and with practice can be advanced by even the most unbelieving executive. The best driver to make that an easy process is a genuine interest in other people!

When I am invited to do Master Classes in coaching, I use a lot of reflective language for the reasons above. Often, someone in the audience will say, following a coaching demonstration, that my coachees[6] must have noticed the unusual way I was talking. We then turn to the coachees and ask **them** what they noticed. There has not been an occasion when reflective language has been noticed by those individuals. Let's see exactly what I mean in practice.

---

[6] A coachee is the most commonly used term for someone who is being coached.

Tom: *Irene is giving me Hell because I cannot release time for her project – we have our own time-issues. I feel exposed as she has previously used a situation like this to undermine me with colleagues and I only learned of it afterwards. I had to do some damage limitation because she is very plausible.*

Angus: *Tom, may I recap to check I get this right? Irene is giving you Hell because she wants time for her project? You are feeling exposed as she has used a situation like this to undermine you? Is that right?*

Tom: *Twice actually.*

There is a lot more a good coach could do to take this conversation to any one of many productive conclusions. In this case it might just serve to say:

Tom: *Twice! Okay what can I do to help in a nutshell? Or,*

Tom: *Twice! Would you like me to intervene or is there another way forward in your view?*

These both acknowledge that you have heard the double experience. If Tom were struggling you might just offer solutions rather than encourage him to find his own. We will develop a flexible management philosophy for this type of situation in the sections on Motivation[7] in chapter 13. Reflective language comes naturally the more you try. At first, try to concentrate on the nouns and adjectives and that will give you confidence to do more and with good effect.

---

[7] See The McLeod 3 Zone Management Model.

Summary feedback

When you summarize, it is then important to invite feedback to correct any misunderstandings. If your summary agrees with what they feel they told you, then a process of 'summarizing the corrections' and subsequent feedback will be required to be sure that you are both fully on the same page. Where long-term misunderstandings occur, or a pattern of communication that is unproductive is common, you can be sure that one of the issues is that of 'being heard'. The answer to that lies in the use of reflective language to summarize what you have heard and then asking if your summary is correct. The mechanism stops long-term communication issues in their tracks.

Involvement in decisions

In most cases, the people who report to us are able to help us to come to sensible decisions about the way forward. If you are not sure, give them the benefit of the doubt and ask them!

> Tom, if you agree that this outcome is unsatisfactory, do you want to suggest some practical ways for moving forward to avoid this from now onwards?

Their contribution will depend upon their abilities but will encourage more self-starting and hence less of your time in future.

Giving credit for ideas and actions overtly

When you listen well, particularly in team meetings, ideas flow from different people. In the passage of time actions and plans take shape and these lead to success. Honoring contributions is sensible, as we may not know which members of the team are most possessive or proud of their ideas. If we want them to continue being creative and making contributions, then a level of recognition is recommended. At the first stage it can be as simple as:

> *Tom, thanks for that idea, I'm going to write that down on the board.*

Many managers know that the bulk of creative development arises from the quality and involvement of their team. And it can be a nice feeling to be associated very closely with their talent. However, being associated is not the same as taking ownership. In some reports, minutes and communiqués, it is appropriate to mention the originator of the idea, even if that person is not on the circulation list. If it's a success and many people know, the person will hear about it from someone.

As well as the grape-vine, recognition may be due at the annual 1-2-1 or some other 1-2-1 opportunity. These small tokens of respect can be greatly warming to people. Imagine such recognition happening to you.

- Which, if any, of the listening skills we have covered could be development areas for you?

- What will you do to improve your skills?

- Where will you test them and with whom?

ACTIONS

People skill: Understands others

We know that 1-2-1 meetings (including using the Wheel of Work), as well as informal conversations, are helpful to learning about people's motivations. Quite a lot is also given away in language. I have been urging increased use of language skills and acute listening, as both will help to develop a greater sensitivity to the words people choose to use and the stress that they place on those words. This will not only increase your perception of the meaning behind the sentences, but also impact on their level of motivation and demotivation. The same applies to commitment.

> We are a day behind schedule. There have been supply issues and I am not at all happy that the data-loggers were not in place. I think we can catch up if the delayed parts are here this morning.

One person's 'not at all happy' is another's 'I am really pissed that you did not approve the purchase of the data-loggers last month. If you had, we would now be two days ahead of schedule'.

That project is going okay. Oh, I'd like to talk with you about the car plan for next year.

The word 'okay' has no passion in it. It's a low-energy word. This, coupled with a change of subject to something else, suggests that there is more we need to know and so should ask questions to isolate what is missing. Is it motivation, commitment, or is something going wrong with the project itself?

As well as language, there is the aspect of the Real Thing – authenticity. Is what they say believable or not? Sometimes the instinctive feeling you have is more accurate than the logical (but sometimes not[8]). If a person you know says in a flat monotone, with no animation at all,

I am really excited about the prospect of running this project

Then you can be quite sure that that person is not excited.

Underpinning these skills is flexibility in both approach and action. Without flexibility, the capacity for leadership is severely hampered.

People skill: Supportive (TF)

Being supportive is a trust factor. Support that is encouraging in both words and action increases the allegiance of people.

---

[8] We look at the development of instinct about others in Part Three when we consider Emotional Intelligence.

Of course, this support also needs to come from a real desire to support and needs to be appropriate to each individual. This may be something you do outside the context of work but have not yet applied more widely at work.[9] But don't fake it! People generally sense dishonesty even if they cannot analyze why they feel that way. It is better, therefore, to avoid acting and provide support only to those whom you genuinely feel some affinity for. We shall come back to this in the chapter 'The Real Thing at Work'. The support skills cross-over with those of listening. To support well you need to listen well. Your support will be encouragement for their initiatives and can involve physical support – provision of an assistant, a quiet area, or time for reflection and so on. It is also likely that you will check in to see how they are doing and this checking-in needs to be thoughtfully carried out since it can easily be misinterpreted as over-managing. To get the balance right have conversations and ask questions.

> Tom, I'd like to check with you that you are getting the right level of information and support from me at this time, also to consider any up-coming change as your new project comes on-stream.

The willingness to give support makes a tangible statement that you care about that individual in a professionally acceptable way. This attends to the varying 'security' needs of people. If they are not worrying about their security they can work with more focus and higher productivity. Small gestures of support may thus have long-term benefits.

---

[9] The concept of transforming behaviors from outside work into work contributes much to the discussion in Chapter 19: 'The Real Thing at Work'.

People skill: Interested in me (TF)

This skill also makes the same tangible statement, attends to varying 'security' needs and offers the same long-term benefits.

However, being interested in people is not quite enough to get benefit from this important trust factor. We need to exhibit the behaviors that arise from genuine interest to maximize the impact. The great management guru, Dale Carnegie, focused on these skills in his seminal book, *How to Win Friends and Influence People*. Here are some thoughts of my own:

- Have social conversations and remember details such as names of family members, hobbies, interests – especially those in which the person shows animation or excitement.

- Recall detail such as when and where they are going, or went, on holiday and ask afterwards about that holiday.

- If you give gifts, make that gift personal to their interests.

- Listen and ask questions – they should be doing more talking than you.

- Be genuine.

- Have more face-to-face meetings and use more hand-written notes rather than relying on e-mail.

- If you share an interest or passion, share that with them but beware of one-upmanship and be brief.

- Mix at coffee-breaks and meals, avoid the cell-phone.

- Be unhurried, slow the pace; even if you have pressures, let those go for the duration of the conversation.

Do any of these ideas or any of your own lead to specific actions?

Where, when and with whom will these take place?

ACTIONS

11

Other influencing skills of the leader

THERE IS MORE TO INFLUENCING PEOPLE THAN ALL THE qualities of the leader described up to this point. We must note that influence can also be applied without rapport through control structures. For example, it is possible to establish strategies and tactics that favor certain people without requiring any sort of relationship with them. These skills owe more to politics and power-play than the more modern skills of managing and leading people (to encourage them to follow you). Here, we will concentrate on the power of influence using interpersonal skill sets – those used by business leaders to create successful people-networks that make things happen. We have considered the skills of building rapport and trust in relation to influence. Now let us look at another set of personal skills. These will include accommodation, compromise and collaboration. Later we will also look in more depth at motivation, as an understanding of motivation provides the key to knowing how to influence people.

Accommodation, compromise and collaboration

These are three of the five 'conflict' traits described by Thomas and Kilmann (1974) in their commercial model. The other two are 'competing' and 'avoiding', which cannot normally be considered as leading-strategies. However, competing and avoidance need to be recognized so that appropriate responses can be made.

Competing and avoiding cannot be viewed as holistically valuable in organizations but will arise from others around you. As leaders, we firstly need to be able to recognize when others are taking a competitive stance or have backed away. In both cases, if it is useful to us or the organization, we need to try to engage and influence them at a more positive level. If we do not try, then nothing will happen. The '51 percent' rule applies:

> In any given interaction I am 51 percent responsible for the outcome of that interaction.

Dealing with competing

Competitive positions are not always blatantly obvious. What do you analyze from this?

> As you know, my position has always been very clear about corporate gifts and kick-backs.

The word 'always' is an obvious hot-word. The word 'very' suggests a high level of emotional attachment to their position/value, and the way in which the word 'my' is used will also give clues to the level of immovability of the individual concerned. If he or she appears to be stressed then you can bet that you have a fight on your hands. Having recognized a competitive position there are two important steps to be taken if you are to have any chance of making progress. The first is most important.

1. Acknowledge the person's position.

2. Encourage the person to gain perspective outside his own position.

The form of acknowledgment might sound like this:

> Tom, your position on corporate gifts and kick-backs have indeed always been very clear and I want to thank you for that. In this case I think you might be able to provide some advice and direction because of some special factors. Can I share those with you and ask for your suggestions for moving forward?

To gain perspective we might ask a number of questions, but the first part of that will be to provide information:

> Tom, Dr Fairmount met with five of the stakeholders at his own expense and as a result we have the extraordinary potential of getting agreement to the merger. He has also told us privately that he is willing to appear as an expert witness at the commission in order to support our case.

And this may be followed by a question asking for a change in his perception:

> Do you know people who would be motivated by receiving a token gift to honor their work for us?

Can you think of a suitable way to signify our thanks?

If you were in Dr Fairmount's position, would you have done those things for this company?

I avoid the question asking him what he might expect if he had done what Dr Fairmount had done on the basis that if he walks-his-talk, he would not want to receive a gift for his efforts. We will see later that we might be able to lead Tom to one of the three leadership strategies.

Dealing with avoidance

Recognition of avoidance is obvious if it is your face:

There is no way I will have anything to do with this, period.

But avoidance is often not recognized because the issue has retreated out of near vision. If the issue is important, the awareness will come back. If you suspect avoidance what can you do? Firstly, check out the situation:

Tom, I was sort of expecting you to come back to me regarding the Flite Project. That may be my error? Are you intending to update me and if so when will that be?

The leader will recognize that these new commitments may also be ignored. A decision then has to be made about the level of interaction needed to get a result. In both cases it may be helpful to help the individual to have a clearer understanding of the implications for him from two different aspects. These represent the stick and carrot of motivation:

1. What is detrimental to him in not moving forward?

2. What are the potential benefits to him of moving forward?

Conversations might then go something like:

> *Tom, what do you imagine the Directors will think of you if the Flite Project gets behind target?*

> *Tom, what do you think your colleagues and I will think of you if Flite runs smoothly to time and budget?*

In this particular case, the issue may be about the relationship with Tom. Again, if we do not ask the question we may not find a way forward:

> *Tom, the fact that I have asked for updates on Flite and you have not come forward suggests to me that you may have an issue with me as your manager. If that is the case then I hope you agree that the professional thing to do is to discuss that and move forward?*

This may not be the issue but a frank question like this and a willingness to work with the person ought to encourage a more fruitful conversation in which the root cause of the issue comes to light.

Let's now look at the three leadership strategies: accommodation, compromise and collaboration.

Accommodation: Building credits

When we accommodate, we give part of our desire or objective away in order to satisfy the other person. This can be seen as weak since we are gaining nothing in return, just losing something. However, small accommodations can also be seen simply as favors and may have a longer-term benefit if used wisely. An example might be giving up an hour of your holiday time to edit the report of a colleague. This does not necessarily make you a doormat, but may make a friend of a colleague. Sometimes it is helpful to overtly give way and call in your investment at a later date. This has a place in management because it creates a tangible tie between you and the other person. The bigger the accommodation, the bigger the favor you might call in when you need it.

If you help your colleague during your holiday, you are sending a clear message: 'You owe me one!'

As leaders we must be able to recognize an offer to accommodate us and remember that, if accepted, we may need to give way to them at a later date in order to maintain rapport. Things are rarely free.

I'd be happy to do that for you on this occasion.

This is not ideal for me but I am willing to let you have Tom for that week.

Both statements give the clue that personal loss is at stake. Here is one that does not:

Okay, I'll do it Frank.

If their statement does not provide clues then you need to be more sensitive to the needs of others to recognize that you have gained something from them. We shall return to those skills in Part Three where we look at Emotional Intelligence.

Compromise: Trading for success

In compromise, both parties trade-off part of their individual objective in order to make some (limited progress) but, importantly, to maintain or improve the quality of their relationship. This is analogous to haggling, where people may trade-off individual objectives to achieve a bargain. A business example might be to give an additional two days leave to one of your staff provided that the individual stays late on Friday evening to help to put a presentation together. You both give a little, but both gain also. If the trade is fair to both parties then there is no outstanding credit to be paid off. But you have the advantage of having done it once, and this leaves the door open to trading by compromise again.

Compromise ought to be fairly obvious to spot:

> *I have submitted my bid for the new plant and will be willing to reduce my overtime costs by 5 percent if this can be approved in this financial period.*

If you have a situation where someone is competing then you might wish to encourage him to compromise as this is a relatively small step for him to take, assuming that he will get some benefit from what you have to offer:

> *Tom, I hear where you are coming from but cannot go as far as you want on the lead-time. If we could agree on five weeks rather*

than four, I would be willing to discuss with you an early-payment incentive of one percent for BACS payments within 21 days of invoice.

Collaboration: Partnering for creative solutions

When we collaborate there is a chance that both parties will gain from the process. This really is a win-win strategy. If someone is competing then there is a better chance of having him compromise than collaborate, at least to begin with. Collaboration works on the foundation of rapport and trust, and those who are in competition with us do not have that, whatever our own value in the relationship may be. Someone who is avoiding, however, may be doing so because he feels undervalued. In that case, an offer to invite him to collaborate with you (as an equal) might work very well rather that deal-making via compromise.

When we collaborate, we are **both** seeking to find outcomes that provide the best win-win for us. The result of collaboration may or may not be better than a compromise. If both parties are creative and trusting there is a chance that the solution will be mutually beneficial. Naturally, that requires risk by both to be more open-handed. An introduction to collaborate might go like this:

Tom, the Board has decided to cut six percent overhead from the whole of my Division. It's a company-wide initiative to drive costs down. Head-count is the obvious answer in your area and I could ask you to do just that. I wonder, though, if we could work together to find solutions that give the best possible result

in terms of retaining competences, succession, team-spirit and
so forth – will you work with me on this?

We all have these three skills but we can learn how to use
them more effectively.

Our colleagues will often provide us with clues to what they
are looking from us during negotiation. These may be more
or less overt. If we can take risks, build rapport and trust, we
can move them toward collaborative solutions.

Recognition

We have had examples of recognition in the sections above.
Look at the following and then decide whether the person is
expecting to compete, avoid, or one of the three leader strategies of accommodate, compromise or collaborate:

1. *Things are at fever-pitch at the moment and it is just*
    impossible to provide the time of any of my team to help
    with the project in your area. Could we find another way
    around these issues?

2. *I'll get around to that. Oh, your pen has fallen on the*
    floor.

3. *This week? I'd be happy to help but the situation is that*
    I do not have any spare capacity at this time and cannot
    produce that product this month.

4. *If you can provide me with initiatives that will gain*
    another 5 percent on overhead-recovery then I would be

prepared to invest twice that amount for the equipment you want.

5. *I'll complete these and send them out, you get off home – you have a big day tomorrow.*

The answers are given in the footnotes.[1]

In negotiation, things are generally much more subtle. What about this phrase:

I'm not sure we could go as high on discounting

This is not accommodating but suggests that a compromise might work if the other party is willing to trade-off. In fact, coming back with a collaborative exploration to meet any other needs the person may have, for example, a longer-term contract, might also be a welcome approach and provide the basis for finding a wider range of solutions that have increasing benefits for both parties. Of course, you would need to test that interpretation and ask a question. For example:

Okay, I get the feeling we might both make headway here and would like to try. But, I am wondering whether there is a more creative solution than looking simply at price? Is there something we have not discussed where we might help or give you some comfort, perhaps a longer-term call-off contract enabling you to gain some bulk discounting on your own purchases?

---

[1] 1. Collaboration; 2. Avoidance; 3. Competing; 4. Compromise; 5. Accommodation.

If the individual is not willing to play the collaborative game, he may simply say.

> *Sorry, but no. Our goods-in volumes are already so high that costs are as low as they will go.*

If he wishes to play, then he might say:

> *Well, thank you. We would not expect any savings with our current high volume turn-over with this product line. However, a call-off contract does help with our logistical planning, especially if you could agree to take product every month. We might agree what the minimum monthly take-off to help us might be without creating the burden for you of high stock inventory.*

Whether the conversation leads to a result is almost irrelevant. Once the process of collaborative work starts, both parties are gaining rapport and trust (through sharing of preferences) and this will lead to a better solution for both of them.

12

Mindsets for leaders

W E HAVE PUT FORWARD THE NOTION THAT A MINDSET is simply a set of values, beliefs and a sense of self that help (or hinder) in a given situation. In effect we are preparing ourselves for who we will become by taking on the psychological state that is productive for us. That will be a deeply personal and unique thing, not something I might give you. At the beginning of each day, as part of a few moments of reflection, you might then wish to bring your thoughts to your mindset for leadership. This calming and centering of focus, based upon self, helps to set up the best possible attitude for starting the day.[1]

---

[1] There are many detailed methods for the process of achieving positive mental states and I leave it to the readers to develop their own sense of what is right for them. For those who wish to know more I refer you to the NLP literature in particular and also mention the process of anchoring. Anchoring allows state-change to be created in an instant. In fact, if you go through the same process of running through your own mindset as detailed, you are likely to arrive at the same place. Anchoring is often referred to in the NLP literature, including McLeod (2003).

From all the chapters on leadership to date, you will be able to collect a set of statements. From that you may be able to form one key thought that crystallizes all your thinking about leadership into one sentence, metaphor, symbol, archetype or totem.[2]

See if you can put together your own personal values, beliefs and sense of self that for you epitomize leadership. If you have a representation of that (which might even be a musical phrase) then also think about using that as part of your mindset for your own personal style of leadership.

MY MINDSET FOR LEADERSHIP

---

[2] Metaphor is simply a story that has an analogous meaning. An archetype might be a mythical leader like Gandalf, a symbol might be an icon or logo that represents a key quality of leadership. A totem is very often an animal used to represent the qualities that we believe are important.

13

Motivation

MOTIVATION IS ENTIRELY BASED UPON THE understanding that people have individual motivations and individual demotivations, and knowing what these are for each person in the work context. In Part Three we will see that understanding other people (and their motivational drivers) develops from understanding self. The understanding of self has two components: growth and change. The growth is in self-awareness and the change is in belief and action (as a result of that awareness).

Understanding self and understanding others are, fortunately, both advised by feedback. For that reason alone, a policy of directing or managing appears rather fruitless. A flexible approach, involving people and facilitating their potential, creates a much improved climate for productive work. One of the biggest errors widely made by managers is that of under- and over-managing. Can you think of times when these happened to you? Over-managing and under-managing create stress, unproductive thinking (for example, internal conversations) and unproductive behaviors. We do not like it. The people who work for us also dislike it.

Motivation: Under- and over-managing

At management development and leadership trainings, I often ask delegates whether they recall being subjected to either of these two extremes. There then follow nods and the sharing of past and present experiences. Uniformly, delegates agree that the effect of both under-managing and over-managing is the same. They are demoralizing, demotivating and have a negative effect on productive work. In an instant then, it ought to be possible to make major changes in the productivity of any team by attending to just this one aspect of management and doing it well. I believe that to be the case.

> *Intelligent and flexible use of different managing styles will produce more productive work than one style.*

This is one of the reasons that must have encouraged Ken Blanchard to develop his Situational Leadership Model many years ago. This suggested four styles of managing (not leading) based upon two observations: the individual's level of competence in that work situation and their level of commitment. These two factors alone determined the level of explicit direction and or support that a manager should give. There has been at least one change in the nomenclature of the model over the years, but the designations still seem at odds with the world today; specifically the interchangeable use of the words 'leadership' and 'managing' and the odd use of the word 'coaching'. All these words now have more specific meanings than they had then. Even so, the model helpfully suggests that intelligent and flexible use of different managing styles will produce more productive work than one style. This belief is a powerful place to start. If you come to work and manage in one way, you are missing tricks.

To manage flexibly we will also need to communicate flexibly.

Perception, test and action

As managers we get used to reading signals, making assumptions, and acting on those remotely. The danger in that strategy of managing is that it is inflexible. If we make assumptions and get those assumptions wrong, then we are likely to demotivate.

Instead, it is helpful to have another system of choice available. This is 'Perception, Test, Action'.

The perception stage is simply what you already do, read the signals. In practice, the step, 'test' means asking a question that may be as simple and as fast as this:

I'm noticing that you are busy and popping in to see me less, is there any support or advice I can give to help you now or later?

The question is phrased to suggest a number of things:

- I notice

- I care

- I trust you, but don't let me down!

- I am still managing and focused on results

- I am willing to support you flexibly

- I am willing to provide knowledge if you need it

- You might not want these now but the offer remains open.

Contrast this with typical manager interventions:

> *You have not reported in this week. Are you on target? Do you need anything?*

This intervention may indicate a number of things. One interpretation might be:

- I notice

- I care

- Don't let me down

- I am still managing and focused on results

- How little might I do now.

Or worse:

> I've noticed that you seem to be overloaded so I have assigned
> the Mojo Project to Simon as of now.

The intervention could be interpreted thus:

- I'm right

- I manage

- If you don't like it, that's tough, get on with your job.

I believe that it is better to adopt a style of questioning that
involves the individual in the solution and enables him to
correct any misinterpretation.

For example, when asking this question:

> I'm noticing that you are busy and popping in to see me less, is
> there any support or advice I can give to help around this time?

The answer might be:

> Oh, sorry. No. I am up to date with all actions. I just heard from
> Bob that you are incredibly busy with the forecasting review for
> next week's sales conference and did not wish to burden you at
> this time.

Perception is clearly the key to getting our management
pitched at the right level. It is also underpinned by a genuine
interest and concern about people. We will return to the subject
of enhancing ability to perceive and motivate in Part Three.

Testing, in other words the communication that seeks to involve people, avoids the pitfalls of misunderstanding and reduces the likelihood of over-managing or under-managing. If in doubt, ask! Perception, Test and Action.

Motivation: Mentoring and coaching

We are continuing the theme that to manage well, we need more than one style of management, and that must be underpinned by skills and the flexibility to use them appropriately. Sometimes that flexibility will be needed with some people in the space of one short meeting, facilitating them through an issue where they are able, helping them with actual detail and ideas for another issue where they are struggling for knowledge.

Typically, the management of people involves day-to-day maintenance and planning. At the level of individual motivation, managing will involve an adequate level of support and information provision. This involves telling, giving instructions, listening and responding.

Those people who have more independence will need less of your time. Their needs for information and support will still exist but instead of telling them, we can encourage them to step into the Stretch Zone so that they can find their own information and support (and need less management time from you in the future).

More adequate employees – that is, the more experienced and succeeding self-starters – will benefit from another approach that is entirely facilitating: the process of coaching. These people have much of the know-how to do the job but lack only the potential for using their minds more creatively, to look beyond the obvious and to understand the wider implications of decision and action. Let's define these motivational terms and explore them before looking at a model for managing and leading that helps to solve our under-managing and over-managing issues.[1]

The Three-Zone Management Model

Have a look at the core of the Three-Zone Management Model shown in Figure 13.1. The vertical axis is based upon the zone of 'independence' of the person. The horizontal scale shows a developmental curve from the lower levels to the highest, right. We see three zones to the right of the vertical axis. Information and Support in the first 'Management' zone, Mentoring to Seek Information & Support in the second 'Management' zone (where instead of telling, the manager is trying to develop self-motivated thought in his employee) and Coaching for Mental Performance in the 'Leadership' zone where a facilitative approach is appropriate for highly independent employees.

Independence

Individuals are independent when their needs for information and support are minimal. They are capable of doing the work

---

[1] For a fuller description of these skills together with scenarios, please see McLeod (2003).

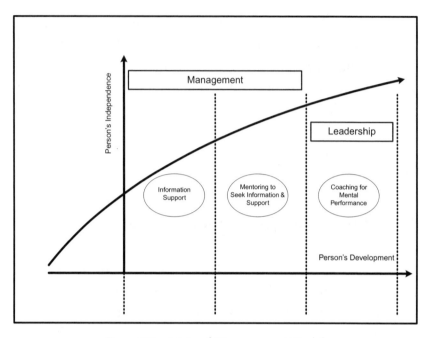

Figure 13.1 McLeod Management Model

and they self-resource themselves to satisfy their needs for information and support in most situations.

At every zone in the model, no unilateral decision is made about the way to manage someone, but rather it provides clues to the sort of conversation we will have to determine the best way forward, for an individual, in that context. This involves dialog and a simple process of Perception, Test and Action.

It is important to know that in zones one through three, a single person may be in any zone in one context at work and then in another zone in a different context at work – each requiring different things from us.[2]

Information and support

Information includes data such as knowledge, how the people-networks operate, how-we-do-things, boundaries and those items from our own developing experience that we need to be easy achievers in our jobs.

Support takes a number of forms. These can include personal recognition, personal acknowledgment, offering to assist, offering to facilitate, providing resources, and boosting confidence and commitment through success or failure.

Mentoring

If someone is not familiar with the job, then we simply need to tell that person what to do precisely, and provide lists of actions and know-how. Mentoring adds to this since it involves less direct information and widens the input of information to include examples and stories – to offer new ways of thinking, new choices rather than instructions. One can go further, where an individual is independent enough, questions can be used to encourage them to find new perceptions, new choices and motivated actions.

---

[2] For readers who are familiar with the Situational Leadership model of Ken Blanchard, this will come as no surprise – the response needs to follow the individual's needs. Here, though, great influence is given to testing one's perception directly with the individual before acting upon that perception.

All of these can be linked:

> *Tom, I can think of three options we might use here and these are <gives details 1, 2, 3>. There may be at least one more I haven't thought of. Would you like to think of other options and then discuss the pros and cons of each?*

> *Tom, I had a similar problem some years ago and at the time came up with an idea. This was <gives detail>. In addition, I can think of another two options <gives details A, B>. Do any of these give you ideas for what to do now or is there a better way?*

The process provides information to the relative novice in a culture to understand what and how things are done within the culture, and encourages independent thinking so that he may need less of your management time in the months to come. There is a good reason for providing ideas and solutions in threes (see McLeod, 2004). The reason behind this is simple. Where you offer one solution, mentees will typically accept or reject it without further processing. The decision is a simple 'yes' or 'no' based upon their current thinking.

Our minds are adapted to making comparisons. The yes/no tends to stimulate that simple process. When a mentee is given three solutions, the process becomes more complicated. With three solutions, several concurrent comparing steps would be needed:

A to B
B to C
A to C

As the comparisons begin, the mentee will typically give up the comparing process and start to do higher-level processing. Once this happens, it is more likely that he will introduce ideas of his own based upon his own experiences. The result is likely to be a new idea, previously inaccessible to the mentee.

Facilitation

This term is applied to methods of drawing out the latent potential and knowledge in people whether in 1-2-1 or in groups. In this case information is not normally provided, on the premise that the solution needed can be developed by enquiring and by the mentee's self-reflection. This can be neatly illustrated by considering the process of coaching, which is essentially facilitation on a 1-2-1 basis.

Coaching

Coaching is a facilitation process dominated by three 'Principle Instruments', these are Questions, Challenges and Silences. The silences are vital since that is where self-reflection leads to the most motivated breakthroughs.

Questions

Questions have many purposes. Typically at the early stages of an issue or goal development, we use questions to develop perception and choice. Questions include:

- What other options are there?

- And if there was another option, what is that option now?

- And if I had this same challenge, how would you advise me now?

- Imagine you are an observer in that situation, what is happening?

These are all open questions[3] in that the answers require detail rather than a yes or no answer. Later, we may ask questions to get to a single plan of action:

- *Which of your ideas will work best for you and the department?*

After that we will want to test the mentee's motivation and be sure that the plan of action is holistically sound and realistic. Again, questions are used:

- *What are the pros and cons of those options?*

- *How would that be for you if you did not succeed?*

- *What other resources are needed to achieve that?*

---

[3] All these questions fall into a number of other categories as well as 'open'. Also, the opposite type to an open question is a closed question. This can be answered by the words yes, no or a numeral.

- *If there is another implication we missed, what is that?*

- *And if that does mean more work, what about your private life?*

When they are fairly certain and committed to a course of action, it is then useful to use questions again in order to invite them to undertake a sensory journey:

- *Imagine it's all done, you have the award, what is that like now?*

Challenges

Whereas questions may invite a new perspective or action, challenges are more pushing than pulling in nature.

Challenges can be statements or questions and are designed to shift perception to another level. Challenges can only be made where there is already a very good, working level of rapport and a willingness to be pushed further into the Stretch Zone. Remember that the Stretch Zone is also called the learning zone. It is from this zone that new perceptions and ideas will spring.

- *Who says you are hopeless?*

- *Is that slightly hopeless or completely hopeless?*

- *What would someone else need to think, believe and do in order to be that scared?*

Not very good at presentation? I have never seen you present but let's agree that you are really terrible at presenting and move on to the next item.

The more challenging statements only work if the rapport is excellent. Of course you risk rapport every time you push a person into the Stretch Zone but that must not deter you.

Silences

'*Learn to be quiet enough to hear the sound of the genuine within yourself so that you can hear it in others*'
MARIAN WRIGHT EDELMAN

'*Silence is ever speaking. It is a perennial flow of language, which is interrupted by speaking*'
SIR RAMANA MAHARSHI

We have talked about silence before in Part One when considering the benefits of self-reflection. In coaching, the most profound perceptions and motivations arise because the coachee has been able to self-reflect (without an interruption from their coach/leader). These silences can run for several minutes and the coachee is never aware of that time span because their focus is wholly internal. The self-reflective silence may create a novel solution, great certainty, massive motivation, a great feeling of stupidity for not having thought of the solution before and/or an overwhelming desire to start on their plan instantly. In other words, the most extraordinary convictions and energy arise directly from careful questioning and a silent space in which they self-reflect.

The coaching-leader therefore needs a number of key skills to work at this level of performance. These skills include questioning skills, rapport-building skills and knowing when to stay silent, or better, when to break a silence.

The ability to hold that silent space is one that needs practice and confidence to achieve. We run courses to do just that[4] – looking at the power of silence specifically but also, naturally, to develop all the skills of coaching-leaders.

To begin with, notice these two things:

1. Where there is a silence and you have an urge to break it.

2. When you ask a question and a silence follows.

If you have discomfort with silence then it is worth while giving yourself permission to stay with silence, and practice by leaving longer silent spaces in conversations. If a person is busy thinking through an answer to your question, then force yourself to be quiet and observe the effect of that.

Silence is enormously powerful. It can be used to help people to talk themselves into uncomfortable reality; for example, that they and not their people are responsible for some event that went badly. Silence is also powerful when used just prior to speaking at meetings – the more confident and impressive you are, the longer the time that you can hold

---

[4] The Power of Silence, first designed and delivered with Steve Breibart.

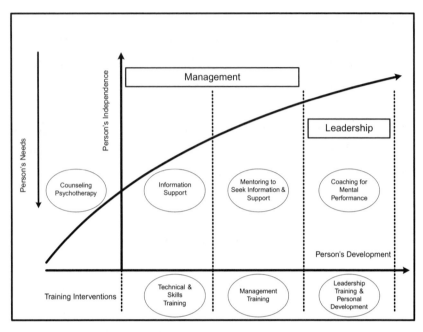

Figure 13.2 Extended McLeod Management Model

that silence. This increases your status in the perception of others.[5]

Working with the Three-Zone Management Model

Now look at the extended model given in Figure 13.2. This includes a new zone to the left of the vertical axis and a number of training interventions that support each zone in the model.

---

[5] This is an area of expertise of John Abulafia, the operatic director and trainer.

For completeness, the off-chart Zone 0 (to the left of the vertical axis) is shown. This zone is where additional help and support is normally required by some individuals. Not only are they lacking independence but, as we see, their level of need (particularly emotional needs) is very high. Although outside the area of normal managing per se, many of us have experiences of people who, for one reason or another, descend into a psychological state where they are no longer really capable of effective work (at all times) without specialist support. As managers, we must be able to distinguish the point at which help is needed and react accordingly – hence its inclusion now.

When we manage, it is more important to understand the best way we might manage rather than be able to label someone as being in a particular zone of development. For that reason, I concentrate on the ***differences*** between the zones. Noticing those differences then help you to have productive conversations with the individual so that your response is optimal for their performance. This is flexible managing at its best and will avoid under- and over-managing. To recap, the zones run from 0, 1, 2 and 3 from left to right.

Zone 0 to Zone 1

The differential between Zone 0 and Zone 1 is determined by the emotional resource of the person to do their job rather than by their competences. Competence will help people in both levels to gain self-esteem and self-confidence. However, in Zone 0 the individual is too distracted, too panicky and/or too preoccupied to learn quickly enough and to achieve a consistent level of quality. I have taken Zone 0 off to the left of the main chart because most managers are not qualified to deal with such issues even if they have the time to grapple with the situation.

Zone 0 people have a lack of emotional resource. In its extreme manifestations, this lack of emotional resource can manifest as crying, absenteeism and self-harming. In these cases, it is worth considering having a conversation about further help and involving a professional from the HR department, possibly of the same gender as the person exhibiting those symptoms.

A conversation will allow plenty of time and the manager must always be prepared to go over the same ground several times if necessary. In stress, people may hear but not understand what is being said. This is due to stress and consequent inner-dialogue, self-judgment, interpretation and so forth. When repeating information for them, keep the messages simple and clear.

The conversation will best be conducted in a neutral and familiar space. Ideally they will have options where they can sit without any desk or table between them and you. Make sure there can be no interruptions and that phones are turned off.

> *Tom, I am concerned about you because you seem to be struggling. Because we care about you and not just your work, I have asked you to meet with me so we can talk confidentially about any pressing concerns and issues that you may have. Where we can, I would like us to agree a way forward that will help you to feel confident and competent in your work. To start, would you like to tell me what you believe I have said so far so that we are starting on the same page?*

Asking for clarity is essential. If Tom has gone internal, he will have missed most of what has been said, critically, the part about working together to help him.

Where the emotional situation seems less debilitating it may be possible to have a conversation about some training or 1-2-1 mentoring (from an encouraging colleague) to get their confidence back. Again, an egalitarian space, a choice of identical chairs, and absence of blockage (table or desk) are all helpful. The pace of delivery should be measured and your attention should be concentrated to allow you to observe reactions and gain insight into whether or not they really understand what you are saying.

> *Tom, you seem to be struggling sometimes and I realize that I may have expected too much of you too soon. I want us to talk together so we can both agree a way forward that will get you moving forward and feeling more confident in your work. To start, would you like to tell me what you understand I have said so we are starting on the same page?*

And later:

> *Tom, there may be some options for assisting you to get up to speed faster and I hope that one of them may appeal to you. I am wondering if Joanne or Peter might spend an hour with you for a couple of mornings to offer advice and show you how they do things. Alternatively, you could shadow one of them for a half-day. There is a training course on quality management coming up in two months and I want to put your name down for that as well – how do you feel about these three options?*

In contrast, Zone 1 people do have the emotional resource to improve but need support and information to do that. Not all people at this level will realize that they need help, however – a conversation in all cases makes that explicit. Three things count:

- asking them for their understanding of what you have said;

- asking whether they agree they are in need and, thirdly, if helpful;

- using silence to get that agreement.

Remember that you may have misdiagnosed Zone 0 and Zone 1. The person that you thought was Zone 1 may get upset and their fears, lack of self-confidence, etc., may come spilling out. For that reason, it is still best to make sure that the space is not overlooked, that you have privacy and that interruptions are not possible.

> *Tom, thank you for coming in. I would like you to feel positive about this meeting because its purpose is simply to do our best to advance your working effectiveness and help you feel more confidence as harder projects and more workload come your way. To begin with I would like to be sure we are both on the same page, so could you tell me what you understand I have asked you here for please?*

If any correction is needed to Tom's interpretation, you can give it – use the same phrases as before to make it easier and again ask for his interpretation of what you have said.

> *Tom, I want to tell you that I am pleased with your time-keeping and enthusiasm. I also want to talk with you about some working*

practices that fall short of our requirements in the department – I mean specifically the accuracy of filing and the speed at which files are returned so others can access them quickly. Do you want to tell me what is working and not working for both those issues, I mean the accuracy and the speed of filing?

The speech contains positives and inclusive language ('I also want to talk with you'), is clear and specific but inviting rather than ordering. If Tom does not agree that there is performance issue then resort to specifics and use silence to ensure you get an answer:

Tom, if I heard you right, you disagree that files are being put back incorrectly by you. Here I have five records from three of your colleagues, both the time of your call and your notes in the files are prior to theirs in each case. What do you have to say about that?

Keep the silence unless Tom starts to fidget or to look around the room. We are so used to speech that the silence may be difficult to manage, but you must. A minute – even three or four or more – may be required to get Tom to do the self-awareness work internally so he can realize and admit his errors. If you butt in or argue, all you will achieve is argument. The problem is internal to him and he will not sort that out by arguing his case, only by self-reflection. If he starts to look bored or begins to fidget, ask the same question, just exactly as you did before. The sentence will hit exactly the same processing area in his brain (if it is identical) and no reinterpretation will be required.[6]

---

[6] This comes from understanding about brain function and specifically neural pathways supported by what we know from the use of Clean Language and Symbolic Modeling.

Typically a question like this only needs to be asked once, occasionally twice to get a sensible answer where any amount of argument and denial would have failed.

Angus, I am sorry. I've always struggled with words. I mean, does The Ford Group go under 'T' for The or 'F' for Ford. And what about the Robert Thomas Company? Is that R or T? I thought I put it under Thomas – is that wrong?

Again, the manager will want to gain a mutual agreement about the way forward.

Okay Tom, I could get a print off of all the names in file-order and yes you are right about the difficulties. In the telephone book I have seen the Robert Thomas Company listed under the surname but we list by the first letter of the company name, that's 'R' for Robert'. The list will be useful though as some companies are better known by a brand and that may be at the top of their correspondence, even though we list by company name. An example is 'Whizzo' which is manufactured by the Reading Chemical Company and hence listed under 'R' for Reading. Will that be enough to get you back on track or do you need any other help with this?

At Zone 1 we need to be specific about what needs to be done and how it needs to be done and not offer choices. Choices are only likely to confuse at this time as the consequences of each choice is unlikely to be understood. But testing will check any assumption.

Zone 1 to Zone 2

The boundary between Zone 1 and Zone 2 is demarked by a general change in the level of independent working. At Zone

1 these are largely below professional standards, in Zone 2 they are largely at acceptable levels. There may still be issues about speed, quality or the understanding of the consequences of actions but the base level of work is adequate and advancing. In Zone 2 we can begin to test the person to think solutions through in the areas where he is most experienced. One way to do that is to ask mentoring-type questions.

> *Tom, the Financial Report for Category D purchasing is fine. I want you to look at the circulation list and tell me if you notice anyone that is listed that ought not to be and whether anyone is not listed that ought to be – any thoughts?*

Possibly followed by:

> *Excellent. Now, what do we normally do in a situation like this?*

If Tom does not know the system, you can intervene:

> *Tom, there are at least three ways that might work. The others went yesterday by internal mail right? . . . Okay, we could mail the others with a note from me or you; we could e-mail the report similarly so it catches up, or since all the people we missed have offices that are on site, we could get Jonathon to walk them around by hand with a note. Which do you think would be most appropriate and why?*

The questions are only asked if an assumption can reasonably be made that the individual has some level of understanding in that context, if not, we should consider him as being in Zone 1 and ask what information-needs he may have. The answer to that should be sufficient to enable him to complete the job. We can always test for clarity with another question.

Zone 2 to Zone 3

Zone 2 to 3 is demarked by a higher level of independence. At Zone 3 the person is self-starting and more resourceful. Zone 3 people are taking new initiatives and finding, from experience, better ways of doing things. The real development that awaits them is mental aptitude. By that, I mean the development of higher reasoning, wider and more holistic understanding of the consequences of their actions, broader ability in initiating and developing relationships (to improve performance) and careful and sensitive handling of both communication and management issues. All of these are stimulated most excellently by facilitating their development using coaching interventions to make the difference.

Coaching assumes that they have the mental resources to find motivated solutions for themselves and enough information about the detail of their specialty, the role of their product or service and their impact within the whole business. Using a combination of questions, challenges and silences, the coaching-leader aims to encourage the person to achieve his goal, gain a wider set of options for moving forward and select one that is effective (and for which the person is suited and motivated). For highly practical learning about coaching in management, please refer to McLeod (2003). Here however, are some typical coaching interventions:

Tom, you say that we cannot produce the order in time, but what if we could? What would we have to do in order to do that?

Tom, if I heard you right you said that Peters dislikes you because he has twice left you off the monthly meeting list. If there was another reason for leaving you off the list then what might that reason be?

Tom, you have suggested three different approaches. Which one is the best and why?

Tom, should we concentrate on what we know we can't do or what we can do?

Tom, imagine if you will that John had this same issue going on with him at the moment. What could you advise him to do?

Tom, what if we had just won the Annual Award, how good would we be feeling right now? What do you think we would have learned that would be useful to us in order to achieve this award again?

Each question is designed to test Tom's present perception and move him to a more useful, performance mindset. More than that, professional coaching develops mental agility and provides new mental strategies that Tom will apply long after he or the coach (or coaching-leader) has moved jobs.

The 1-2-1 meetings

So far, we have considered meetings to deal with issues and gain some clarity about the level of information and support that our people may need. But what of the notorious 1-2-1? This needs to be considered here, under motivation, since, in theory at least, the 1-2-1 ought to be an opportunity to improve motivation. In practice the 1-2-1, and particularly the annual 1-2-1, is often demotivating. What is your own experience? Let's illustrate what I mean by including both standard 1-2-1 issues and ordinary 1-2-1 issues that occur in the day-to-day operation.

Within the constraints of our reward and recognition protocols, how might the annual review process be more rewarding for all concerned? That is one of the themes for this chapter.

Some readers will have existing corporate policies for annual performance reviews with (or without) personal development planning. The feedback we receive suggests that these annual 1-2-1 reviews are usually unsatisfactory to manage and less than satisfactory to be subjected to. Senior managers complain that their annual 1-2-1 reviews are always late, often postponed at the last minute, sandwiched between other matters of the day, and of limited duration and limited help. Many complain that their own agenda for the annual 1-2-1 is not requested, and nor is it welcome.

Really this should not be. Let's start with the situation with running 1-2-1s and annual 1-2-1s (annual performance reviews) with our own people and then move to consider handling our own 1-2-1s or annual 1-2-1 with a boss. This will lead us naturally to considering other managing-the-boss scenarios.

Facilitating all 1-2-1s

Whether the purpose of the 1-2-1 is a day-to-day issue, project review or annual performance review, the basic principles are the same. By facilitation I mean the teasing out of information and encouragement to take a lead rather than give direction. The purpose in this is simply to engage the person at a different level – nearer to a collaborative (and supportive) process geared toward improved working performance. Clearly if the individual is fresh to the business then one needs to test the level of facilitation into which they can enter.

> *If something does not work, try something different!*

The manager may sometimes be faced with an individual who is pushing for promotion or additional salary and is either borderline or above the requirement but where, for fiscal reasons, the manager is unable to do anything about the salary or status. In that case some managers will use the 1-2-1 as an opportunity to expose weaknesses and hold down any promotion and reward. One understands the motives but must question whether there is not a better way to harness an individual rather than slap him down and expect him to continue working efficiently.

In cases like this, the manager must dig deep and try very hard to answer the question, 'How can I conduct this 1-2-1 in spite of any limitations, so that he leaves more motivated than he came in?' This should not be too difficult since the person is probably not looking forward to the 1-2-1 in any case. The ideas below will, I hope, give some practical guidelines for trying something different.

The leader will generally wish to adopt a facilitating style in 1-2-1s to increase involvement, to make the individual feel properly heard, and to show own interest and concern. The process of facilitation will also lead to better decisions. But are there situations where the old methods are best? For example, in a situation when, due to hardened and inflexible conduct over the longer term, an individual is expected to respond badly.

Employee reluctance

Most of my readers have teams of people that have worked for them for different periods of time. Some of those relationships carry baggage that manifests as unhelpful, patterned behaviors by them and by patterned behaviors by the manager. In this case my adage is:

If something is not working, then do something different.

Patterns in relationship fire off one another. Gestures, words and intonations trigger familiar responses. If you break your half of the pattern and do it consistently, the other party has to think of an option. It may be shaky for both of you, but it will be different. That must be a good thing, as an existing stalemate situation is typically of low productivity due to the lack of team dynamics. Any difference is probably better than the status quo.

In this type of situation, would it be worth asking if the individual would like to talk you through the 1-2-1 process, rather than the other way around? That might take him off his guard and interrupt any pattern. If you recall, when we want to break ingrained patterns, it is best to interrupt the pattern at the start. If you expect him to shrug and say something like, 'That's your job isn't it?', then you might pass the ball back firmly again,

> *Here is a list of the topics we need to go through. Pick any one you like and go from there in any order you like.*

This is one of those times when silence is your best friend. Do not break it. If the person gets distracted after a time, just repeat what you said and wait.

Here is a scenario where a 28-year-old Plant Manager, Ephrain, is meeting with a 55-year-old Quality Executive, Ted, who has been with the company many years. Ted is typically short with everyone in authority but particularly so with his manager. The manager is uncomfortable with Ted and has to bite his lip to prevent him saying what he really thinks. Ted rarely does anything for him within the required time-frame, creating more stress for Ephrain.

Ephrain:	*Ted, I want you to get the procedures manual finished in time two weeks before the inspection, October third. The draft will need to be checked by Isobel I believe?*
Ted:	*Right.*

Ephrain:	*So you will do that?*
Ted:	*Yeah, is that all? I have a job to do.*

The manager is left with the distinct impression that he will not get his way. Is there a chance that a different method might work? On the basis that in this situation trying something different might be useful, please imagine the same situation but where Ephrain prepares himself mentally before starting, together with a new approach. Ephrain imagines a positive outcome. He decides to breathe calmly and detach himself from the situation, almost like an observer. He does not pressurize himself to be successful but to have a different experience with Ted whether he achieves his outcome or not. Instead of sitting glued behind his desk, he meets Ted at the door of the office and shakes his hand, leans on his desk and then, looking him in the eye says:

Ephrain: *Ted, please sit or stand as you wish, I do not mind. The company needs to get through the quality inspection and so I would like you to talk me through the steps you believe are necessary to be successful.*

Ted: *They are obvious aren't they?*

Ephrain: *So, please talk me through the obvious steps and the less obvious steps that you believe are necessary to be successful.*

Ted: *The manual will need formatting from my document and your secretary does not have any time for my work, so that will probably let us down.*

Ephrain: *So, if your document is formatted quickly for you, how soon exactly will you have the document ready for him?*

Ted: *It depends on other demands from the plant, your people keep trying to get non-specification product past me.*

Ephrain: *Allowing for the current demands and product issues, and if your document could be formatted quickly for you, how soon exactly will you have the document ready for him?*

Ted: *Friday, close of play.*

Ephrain: *Thank you, I will let Robert know and ask him to turn that around as a priority, putting it out to a specialist if necessary and then I will get back to you myself with a completion date. Is that acceptable to you?*

Ted: *Sure.*

Ephrain: *I would like to find mutually satisfactory ways of reducing the loss of your time by the movement of non-specification product. If you will undertake to provide a document, or dictate it to my secretary, then I will study that and we can then agree a strategy for dealing with the issues together.*

Ted: *Mmmm.*

Ephrain: *Do I have your agreement to provide the document for me and to work together to deal with the quality issues on the plant?*

Ted: *Okay, but I must go now, my three o'clock appointment will be waiting.*

Ephrain: *I will not keep you from your appointment Ted, just let's put a time-frame around the document and whether you will prepare or dictate?*

Ted: *I'll do it at the weekend. You will have it Monday first thing.*

Ephrain's first attempt might not go so smoothly but the dialogue illustrates many of the qualities of communication that we have been highlighting to date. It is respectful, inviting and repeats Ted's own phrases which is the 'Broken Record Technique'.[7] Ephrain's first sentence is a totally new departure for him and that is important to mark out the scenario as being different. He is insistent on asking for

---

[7] The Broken Record Technique works because it prevents semantic arguments about the linguistic interpretations of newly introduced language.

an agreement rather than telling. He does not miss anything important and he reflects any language that Ted expresses.

Headline rules of engagement

Think of any bad experiences you or others have had in relation to the 1-2-1. They are likely to include some of the following experiences:

- They put off the meeting twice

- Three months overdue and still no meeting

- Ten minutes only with the boss talking at me

- Would not listen to my point of view

- Would not look me in the eye when he talked about my (disappointing) grading

- Promoted a graduate colleague with less experience or ability

- Signed letters and took telephone calls during the meeting.

These examples are very common indeed. A boss who postpones a 1-2-1 is saying, 'You are not my first priority. I am too important and busy to see you. I do not care.'

It is clear that many companies implement 1-2-1 strategies without attending to the competence level of their managers first – as a consequence, many of the potential benefits of the system are lost – it becomes a demotivating methodology for recording meaningless data and holding the salary overhead down. In my view, if any manager has not been trained and assessed in both role-play and in actual 1-2-1s, the 1-2-1 should be conducted by someone else who has – by professionals who have the competences to do the job properly. I suspect that this would be welcome by a majority of the managers who feel inadequate in running all or some of their 1-2-1s. As leaders, we can do better than that, even if training is not immediately available. Here are some guidelines.

The basic rules of engagement must include the following:

- Time-table all 1-2-1s to meet (or exceed) expectations and keep buffer-time for any restructurings.

- Do not adjourn meetings; if you have to postpone try to have the meeting on the appointed day and apologize in person for the delay, face-to-face; come out of your office to do that or meet the appointee at his domain rather than yours.

- Take the 1-2-1 seriously, do not sandwich it.

- Get your hand back in, if necessary by handling some easy 1-2-1s first.

- Do not leave the hardest ones to last – they know what you are doing.

- Create a positive mindset for good outcomes whatever your past experience may have been.

- Be calm.

- Slow the pace right from the start (put at ease).

- Use a private space, preferably not your office.

- Do not permit any interruption for any reason whatsoever, except fire!

- Offer any of the seats available before staking a claim to any place yourself (with papers or other materials).

- Ask that cell-phones be turned off.

- If you must have a table, both sit at one corner – no barriers between you.

- Budget for more time than you think necessary (reduce pressure on yourself) and leave some minutes for note-taking and reflection afterwards.

- Remember: a start, a middle and an end!

- Select a subject for the beginning that, if work-related, the person is typically very calm and happy to talk about. Ideally pick a subject unrelated to work.

- Restate the purpose of the 1-2-1.

- Check with the individual that he is ready to start.

- Consider letting him run through the process.

- Summarize and agree understandings.

Starting the 1-2-1

However many times you may have run a 1-2-1 with a person, it is important to set the scene for the current one. It is part of the underpinning messages that says, 'I take this and you seriously'. For me, this would involve simple restating of the purpose and the process. I want to say that my objective is to be supportive, to listen and to hope that they will feel more motivated following the meeting than they did before it. I realize that not every leader is ready for that degree of candor. It is possible, however, that a change toward a more frank approach will improve the results you have had to date. Only you can guess this for each situation. But this ought properly to be a conscious consideration and decision – not falling into what one did before because 'they go okay'. Remember that each person is different and one approach is unlikely to satisfy all the people all the time. Flexibility is a key characteristic of leaders. Moving toward an increasing level of facilitation ought, in most cases, to have a positive impact on the outcome.

Limitations: be straight

You know that you can't give promotions or rewards this year in spite of an individual's better performance. Or you know that he has not made the grade, but you know that he thinks he has. These scenarios are familiar. In these situations what is the sense in hedging? You will gain most respect by getting to the point early in the process. But remember the three parts to communication? There needs to be a start, a middle and an end. The start will level the ground, offer the chance for a non-work chat and let any stress levels dip. The middle will deal with the business, and the end will summarize what you have agreed, including asking them to summarize what they have understood.

So, what might one say in the above two cases. How do these sound to you?

Tom, I wish to be honest with you. I am pleased with the way things are going but have no budget for promotions in your area this year. I doubt that is good news but it's a fact. In a moment I would like to hear how you feel about that but I first want to say that I would like us to discuss what we can both do to help with your advancement – and I hope you would welcome that.

Tom, we may differ on this but I have not heard enough to convince me that you have made the grade due to the area D scores we have discussed in depth <details>. Is there anything more you can add that would correct my perception at this time? <pause> I would like to know how much development you are willing to do in those areas to regain your grading or improve it further. I am also willing to discuss with you, guide you in any way I can, to help you perform at the next level if that is what you want. I can be specific about the behaviors and goals that *will be necessary for that to happen. Do you want to work with me to start making that difference now?*

Clearly any statement needs to be in a language that is reasonably natural for you to be using or test. In each case the aim is to be clear, to summarize, and to express co-work and your support. There will still be some who are not bothered or too close to retirement to give a damn, but hopefully strategies like these will improve the general motivation of most of the people who pass through your hands.

> ***Interpretation may create a dispute over semantics rather than substance***

Remember to listen well, and do not interrupt or argue. Reflect their language where possible (since interpretation by you may create a dispute over semantics rather than substance).

We do not always know what to do about an issue that is raised. One of the methods that many people use to manage the 1-2-1 (rather than facilitate it) is to avoid subjects they feel less competent to handle. Leaders have more courage than that and must also be more resourceful. If you do not know what to do, be honest:

Tom, frankly I do not know what to say about that. From what you have told me this is something you would like resolved and so I want to give it further thought and reflection. I would like us to meet again next week specifically to see if we can find a way forward. Before we move on, is there anything else I should know about this situation that might help me think of things we might do to improve the situation?

Bluffing, hedging and ignoring issues are the methods of the inadequate. They fool nobody except the person who uses them.

Ending the 1-2-1

As we saw in Chapter 8, endings are as important as beginnings and middles. This is the chance to heal any remaining grievances and to make sure that you both leave on the same page. Ideally, ask the person to summarize what has happened. Ask him whether there is anything you can do to support him and why not ask him if he feels more or less motivated than he did before the meeting?

> *Tom, at the start of this meeting I mentioned that one of my objectives was to hope that you would leave this 1-2-1 more motivated than you were before you came in. Would you mind telling me whether we have achieved that or not?*

Even if there is one obvious reason for his disappointment (over which you have no desire or ability to budge), still ask if there is anything else that you might address; you may still make gains in rapport by making small gains mutually, even if the big issue remains unresolved.

New staff 1-2-1

In Chapter 4 we introduced the concept of the Wheel of Work. It is worth considering this again (see Figure 13.3) in the context of new staff because it gives a methodology for understanding, building rapport and showing your broader interest

My Contentment Level with..

Figure 13.3 Typical Wheel of Work

in the welfare of the people who work for you. Most of all, it gives you a process for understanding what will motivate those people.

You can adapt the diagram to suit your own style but a printed-off version takes any heat out of asking sensitive/ personal questions. Using a printed version also allows eye-to-eye contact to be withdrawn naturally and refocused on the Wheel. This can help make the whole process of the 1-2-1 easier for both of you to handle in any context. As with all communications, the same three-part process applies: a beginning to establish working rapport and reduce any stress; a middle in which you both do the work; and an end where you may summarize and/or ask the person to summarize his own understanding for you.

With new staff it will be very important to carefully summarize the whole purpose of the 1-2-1 and seek feedback about the person's understanding as you go through rather than waiting until the end. Give the person a clear idea about how you wish to conduct the 1-2-1 process and let him know what is confidential – who has access to the notes and if hard copy is stored, who has access to that.

The ideal scenario is not to direct the person to any part of the Wheel, but to invite him to rate (0 through 10) all the sections in any order.

> *Tom, here is a model I have been using in 1-2-1s and would like us to use it together too. It gives a number of areas for discussion as you can see written in the segments. In no particular order, would you like to let me know what your contentment level is in all these segments and, if you do not mind, I would like to keep some notes that will be filed with the rest, confidentially, in that locked cabinet.*

Let him know, too, that you will ask questions for clarity of understanding. Use those questions to help him to develop his thoughts, and to challenge him to new perceptions where his own beliefs may not be helpful to his contentment and productivity. Remember that silence may be necessary to enable the person to think things through, and that these silences can last for minutes, even though he may not be aware of that.

The 'right' meaning of each section is not really important. What is important is what the person actually wants to bring to the conversation, and any progress you make as a result of that. It is important to keep your mind open and not try to make the person fit your view of what the sections mean. If you feel able, you may decide to add a section called 'Life Balance' so that you both gain more insight to the relative importance of work and the individual's private life.

At the end ask him for feedback on the process and on how you performed. What did he find useful and what less so? What worked well and what worked less well? The individual will not be affected by any negative ideas that exist in your work-culture.

Understanding stress

Stress is acceptable if short term. Undue stress, especially prolonged stress coupled with loss of sleep, leads to errors and the lock-in syndrome (see Part One). It is worth understanding some of the indicators of stress so that discussion and actions can take place where you see it.

It is quite usual for executives in organizations to have oscillating levels of stress (Figure 13.4, see solid line). Normally, if an individual is coping well, he will be able to get his stress levels down between the incidences of stress in his work. The stress is not always obvious by changes in behavior. Tell-tale signs may include:

- Periodic deafness (due to inner dialogue)

- Gazing into the mid-distance (ditto)

- Errors of understanding (ditto)

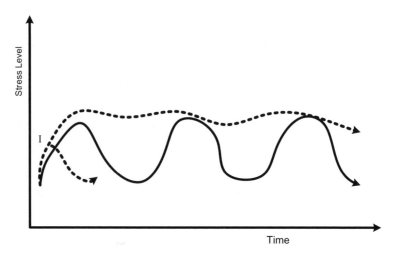

Figure 13.4   Choice and Persistent Stress Syndrome

- Pale, expressionless demeanor

- Ruddiness in the neck

- Stiff jaw and shoulders

- Tics

- Sweating

- Undue persistence

- Clumsiness and forgetfulness

- Errors in work

- Mood swings

- Off-beat comments

- Long working hours

- Uncharacteristic sloppiness in one or more aspects of their appearance.

Where the stress becomes persistent and potentially dangerous to health, the levels of stress do not fully return to normal working levels (top, dotted curve in the diagram). In order to help the individuals, it is useful to get them to understand what the pattern of stress initiation is. This allows the possibility that they may insert a conscious logical thought or question in order to break the patterned response (see lower dotted curve at I).

Stress coaching is very likely to be successful in these situations and clearly a managerial intervention is necessary. Persistent Stress Syndrome (PSS) will lead to productivity problems (some of those listed above) and potentially to more serious psychological and/or health problems if ignored.

Probing the Wheel of Work

The use of the Wheel of Work can be applied for any of our staff, not just new members. You will have the confidence, authority plus any support you may need from peers, particularly in HR. It is enormously useful when we reconsider the dangers of over- or under-managing people and other key motivators and demotivators at work. Skillful attention to the answers will enable fruitful discussion and a positive, motivating outcome for you both.

Rewards and recognition (R&R)

You may or may not have room for movement in the reward package but you can certainly always influence the recognition piece. The recognition that people want can go beyond what you give personally. It may be that a proportion of their work, though critical to the success of a project, may not be overtly attributed to them. Their colleagues may not appreciate their contribution. A mechanism that enabled that recognition among colleagues might be enormously influential in creating motivation. You could, for example, ask them if they would like to contribute to your monthly report (which is then circulated among their peer group). This would give them a chance to report on their contribution in their own words.

With so many people working from home there may be very infrequent face-to-face contacts between colleagues. They may need to meet more frequently as a team where the strengths and weaknesses that the individuals bring to projects can be aired and resolved.

The bold leader is unafraid to get to the heart of the R&R issues:

> Tom, why not tell me how content you are about rewards and recognition?

Relationships

Questions about relationship may reveal issues that may be causing a loss of performance. It could be that people have tensions due to the dilemma of having to satisfy both their direct manager and one or more indirect managers. Or they may have very different managers in various territories, each demanding a different emphasis on effort or result. Airing such issues, encouraging self-starting action, supporting and offering to intervene when absolutely necessary are strategies that can have a positive impact for them. Unless we ask we may miss something like this:

> *All is good except for Thompson who is Project Director in Engineering. She usually waits until you are away on business and then comes in needing something done urgently. This invariably creates tensions in my department and because of her status I do not feel able to refuse her directions. It has happened several times and so I think she now expects it as normal.*

The leader will not deflect from action but must first acknowledge the problem and not make commitments that cannot be undertaken.

> *Tom, I will speak with Ms Thompson myself and then you and I will need to talk so that you have an agreed response should it happen again in my absence. If you can qualify those tensions and any specific issues that have arisen in detail, then that will assist me to get our messages across firmly.*

Work satisfaction

This is a broad area. Remember that the things that satisfy some individuals may be wholly different to your own drivers, but no less important for them.

Factors can include:

- Money

- Flexibility to tackle things their own way

- Ordered processes of working

- Being part of a process

- Seeing things through from start to finish

- Contributing a part in a process

- Working alongside people

- Working productively alone

- Privacy

- Working together as a team

- Meeting new people

- Predictability of the working day

- Variety of each day

- Time-flexible

- Perfection in detail

- Lack of detail

- Fixing existing processes

- Inventing new processes and procedures

- Kudos

- High profile

- Low profile

- Comparative status

- Recognition for expertise

- Recognition for problem-solving

- Recognition for quality and efficiency.

Do any of these summarize your reason for working? If not, what are yours? Why do your immediate colleagues work in the same organization? What aspects of work satisfy the people who work for you? If you look at the list, there are many ways in which a manager can influence the amount of exposure that an individual may have in each area. In other words, we can have a major motivating effect by making small changes in a job (or moving someone to a different job) without changing the salary or regrading. The route to knowing how to do that has to start with knowledge.

> *Tom, what is your satisfaction with work? Here is a list of some things that people find important – are any of these aspects, or any other aspects, really important to you?*

Tom, what could we do to improve your level of satisfaction in that area do you think?

Be prepared to be more specific with questions if the conversation is drying up. Questions could include these:

Tom, what about your working environment – do you get enough uninterrupted time to develop your ideas and produce the detailed manuals?

Tom, to what extent do you enjoy the overseas travel or find it tedious?

Tom, tell me if you will, what are the most important things that make you enthusiastic to come to work?

Remember, too, that you may get more useful information by asking this question:

Tom, thanks for that. I am wondering what, if anything contributes to any dissatisfaction you may have. I wish to see whether there is anything we can do together to influence that?

A leader will have no hesitation about asking this question because we know that motivation and demotivation are the opposing ends of the same dimension. Focusing only on positives is not enough. Sometimes you will be able to do something immediately; sometimes you may not. You might find yourself in this situation:

I am unhappy with the car scheme. I like cars and none of the three on my list are ones I want to be seen in. We are not allowed to pay for an upgrade and the expenses allowed for using one's own car are poor and would cost me a lot.

Unless you have *carte blanche* to do as you wish, you might respond like this:

> *Tom, I hear what you say and I am sympathetic. Clearly I do not make the vehicle-policy here and my influence is unlikely to change the policy overnight, if at all. However, it is likely that others feel the same way as you and so I will bring this to the attention of the Group HR Director and the Benefits Manager and I will blind-copy you. The car scheme at the next level is more interesting isn't it? Perhaps we can focus on a development plan that would improve your chances of getting you to that level – would you be interested to do that?*

This strategy fits in with the concept of focusing Tom where he has impact (Part One) rather on the things where he has little or no impact. By helping Tom to focus on developing his competences we are using his desire for a different vehicle as a motivator for positive change in his work.

Training and development

You may have budget constraints, but an open discussion will reveal areas that can be supported by short-term initiatives other than training. These could include providing literature, discussion time with colleagues, mentoring, free web-based courses and sponsoring evening classes.

Sometimes a person will want tertiary training in something that is not immediately of practical use for his job in terms of skills – for example, personal-development training. Many corporate cultures are rather behind in not appreciating the value of such development among staff – and this may impede you. However, a request like this is an opportunity to widen the discussion and ask about career aspirations. Does the individual want to develop other skills and move out of the organization? Could he be usefully retained in another area of the business following training? If we fail to have this discussion we will not know whether the person is planning to leave. It is much better to know if he is leaving to enable us to prepare for that. And the discussion may open ideas that will turn a relatively unproductive person in the wrong job, into a highly productive person in the right job.

Leaders must be prepared to develop their team even if, as a result, they may lose some of them. Many companies insure against that in the short term by forming agreements of tenure following the training.

A good friend of mine was sent to one of the world's pre-eminent business schools (in Paris) by his company who had no contract to retain him following the training. When the results were posted, three companies made him job offers, each one worth up to three times his current salary. He went back to his company and negotiated a salary more than double the one he was receiving but with a 10-year contract that enabled him to borrow heavily. In that way he enjoyed a lifestyle that he might have had to wait several years for had he continued working on a short-term employment contract.

Many people wish to develop, but preventing them from doing so will not inspire them to be loyal or to work harder than they need to. Leaders will take the problems and expense of losing people because they get better productivity from motivated people. It is also better for the team to be populated by people who are motivated and content than by those who are not. Each negative voice and attitude has a wider effect than that of the individual – they infect the team.

We all know that there are people, often close to retirement, who are not interested in training or anything else other than totting up credits for their pension. What about them? If they have expertise, consider asking them if they would enjoy mentoring a younger member of your staff. If possible we want to find an outlet for any residual enthusiasm that they have. The problem is not going away so we might as well face it head-on. For example, have a discussion specifically about their enthusiasm and what you might do together to improve that. Prepare for the meeting by already having some ideas on how they might contribute something valuable to the business. If they are not good with people, are they good at systems, quality protocols and reports? Ask them outright how they would like to spend a productive day at work?

Amount of change

People's peak effectiveness over time is influenced by the level of security and stimulation they have in their job. The word 'security' is a term used to describe the factors that help an individual to feel secure. Part of that security may be the extent to which they feel part of a familiar culture in the organization. The change that people find acceptable is also a variable at both the micro and macro levels. Some people are not unduly worried by major corporate restructuring but are more concerned that their parking spot and desk are still in the same places. Others are diametrically different to this.

They are shaken by corporate rumors but care more about the people they work with than the location.

The stimulation provided by status quo or by change will be different for different people. Some enjoy variety and will hate to get stuck in one function too long. Others wish to become familiar with a function and expert in its use. That, too, can be a problem in the longer term if we do not get them into the Stretch Zone in some aspects of their job. We need them to retain flexibility for the unknown ahead. Again, we do not know any of these factors unless we have that discussion. The Wheel of Work facilitates that in a wholly productive way.

While we may not be able to make substantial changes to accommodate the individuals, we can at least touch base, factor in other 'security' aspects that make them feel content, and keep them in the communication loop. If we do not, they may become the thought-leaders of negative 'stuff', so it is better to keep them on-side.

Number of major tasks

I have never yet met a manager who has ever asked any of his staff what their ideal number of major tasks might be. When asked for their own preference, these same people will immediately express a figure or range. The answers vary widely and typically from 1 to 15 or more. When I next ask how many major tasks they actually have, the majority usually have a significant gap between their preference and the actual situation. Some people have many more major tasks than is ideal for them – others have too few. Many of both groups often feel overly stressed as a result.

Those people with too few major tasks may need the variety and freedom of work effort that having several projects allows. Security factors may also come into play – a perfectionist may find the stress of putting all his eggs in one basket too high a cost to bear.

You may not be able to take a short-term solution to these problems but a mid-term strategy ought to enable most of us to come closer to satisfying a person's preference, most of the time. The benefits of that go beyond efficiency, of course. You have just brought an individual closer to being touched by your leadership in a valuable and respected way.

Number of reports

The same sort of thinking applies to the number of direct and indirect reports that a person may have, although the manager will normally have quite a good idea before asking the question. Sometimes people want direct reports as a sign of status even though they do not have the temperament to handle so many capably. To avoid that, questioning needs to get underneath any status-issue by asking specifics about their current managing experiences with their people. Get them to talk about their individual reports and encourage them to speak about those relationships and the time they take with each report, the number of 1-2-1s and the outcomes of those in detail. Your own observations will also help you to target your questions to areas of possible concern.

Multiple tasks also appeal to those who need shorter-term successes to maintain motivation. If you have 10 projects, at least one is likely to be near fruition with others following from time to time.

Purpose of my working

This question is also open to interpretation. As leaders, we are really trying to find the biggest drivers of motivation. What do they value about their contribution? Is their focus and enjoyment in today's role, or in the one they aspire to? Ask open questions like:

> *Tom, you say a driver for work is money, but if there is something else, what is that other driver?*

> *What is it about work that makes you feel good?*

> *Tom, if you looked back at your time in this job in 10 years' time, what do you think would have given you the most satisfaction?*

Even if some of these questions seem unnatural for you to ask now, start with a simpler set and gain experience in developing these conversations.[8]

---

[8] See, for example, McLeod (2003).

14

My own 1-2-1

YOU MIGHT ASK WHETHER YOU HAVE ANY CONTROL OVER the format of your 1-2-1 with your boss(es). I know very senior people who have started answering this question negatively by saying that they have no control over their 1-2-1 – it is all in the hands of their immediate boss. Soon afterwards they start to create plans to make some changes to their experience. It seems that many people are unwilling to take the initiative when it comes to their 1-2-1 even though they do so in every other aspect of their work. It is possible that the status and power of the boss is enhanced by the process itself (as traditionally carried out). So, how might one make a difference?

As with all communication we need to set the scene by making sure that there is a beginning, a middle and an end and may need to drive the timing too. The beginning typically starts long before the 1-2-1 itself. Think of the best media for getting your message across. Something like this might be helpful as a model:

Tom, my 1-2-1 is coming up this month and I want to make sure that I and the business get as much out of that in terms of motivation and planned change for greater performance. Could we book out an hour and a half for this somewhere quiet?

Naturally the boss will see this as a coded message that you are expecting an increase in your remuneration package! If previous 1-2-1s have taken 20 minutes, asking for an hour and a half also makes a statement. You may get an hour but it is still three times longer than last year.

Your message may ask whether they mind if you prepare something in advance. Would that be helpful to them and you?

Tom, in addition, I realize that my reports recently have largely been summaries of progress to the Board with little opportunity to talk about strategic possibilities. With that in view, and by way of preparation, I would like to let you have a strategic briefing document during the week before my 1-2-1 with you. Would this be early enough for you or should we delay the 1-2-1 by a week or two?

It worries me that so many people in powerful and influential jobs feel unable, at first, to have this quality of conversation with their bosses. Often this is partly due to the relatively little 1-2-1 time that these people have alone with their bosses, however much time they may have in various groups. It is quite common for people to rarely see their boss alone[1]. Pre-

---

[1] If you are guilty of being largely unavailable for listening to your people on a 1-2-1 basis then imagine how that may affect some of them? They may be privately nervous and uncertain. With those feelings it is likely to affect the scope of their impact and the conviction they have.

vious 1-2-1s may have been very brief, honed in between other tasks. In this case, try the following:

- Request more time from them or the secretary beforehand.

- Immediately before the 1-2-1 request the secretary to ensure that the meeting is uninterrupted.

In many organizations, the Board members are rarely seen 1-2-1 by their executives. In these cases, we tend to project what we observe about their personality in group situations and assume that is how they are in 1-2-1. In fact, Board members are just like us. They do not want to spend all their time feeling isolated or fawned upon – they typically admire straight talking and an opportunity to get under the surface in an open conversation, rather than one that is politically correct and stilted. Like us they want to know that the quality of the decisions they take are based on real fact and that the risks taken are supportable.

Because executives often project their expectations and therefore expect certain behaviors from the Board members, they inadvertently behave in set patterns themselves that, without realizing it, encourage the status quo!

If you want to see a difference then you must behave differently. In this event the strategy must be to test the water bit by bit and see what happens. Any of the following, if different to your current behaviors, might test the possibility of more fruitful relating:

- Prepare with a positive mindset open to new possibilities.

- If they are rushed, say you want the best from the 1-2-1 and offer to restructure and start moving away.

- Take initiatives with the direction of the 1-2-1.

- Be direct and honest, do not hedge.

- Ask questions, 'What do you want to achieve from this process?'

- If there are many chairs, take one at the corner of a table or as far from the desk as possible to encourage a move away from the desk.

- If no summary takes place, provide one to show that you understand what has been discussed and to heal any differences in interpretation.

- If there are short-term actions, request a short-term review.

What new approaches will you now take with your boss if applicable?

ACTIONS

15

Influencing peers and bosses

LTHOUGH THE TYPES OF CONVERSATION AND communication are generally different, the component skills we have introduced are the same. As well as individual differences there may be cultural traits that help you to guess how best to get people on-side. The French, for example, seem to formulate their decisions during coffee breaks or over lunch. Building of respect and a longer-term record of your reliability and trustworthiness may be more important to a Japanese. Failing to keep your word with an Arab may severely limit your influence since your word is often considered to be as binding as a formal contract. In all cases, think about the development of rapport and trust. You may wish to consider these too:

- What is their preferred way of receiving information?

- What part, if any, do they like to play in innovation?

- Do they wish to own new ideas as their own?

- Do they enjoy surprises or dislike them?

- Do they like to exert change and influence on things?

- What is most important to them?

- What do they think of you now?

- What will improve that perception?

These are thinking skills, but another way to develop answers to these questions is to imagine being in their position, to temporarily be the boss[1]. When this is done well, the process provides fresh perceptions which can then generate specific actions that may make a difference. In pretending to be the boss, it is useful to physically move to another chair so that each step toward that chair installs more of the boss's mindset, character and physicality into you. In effect you are leaving your own body in order to imagine being in his.

The difference in perception that results can be enormous. You may have believed that Jackie thinks you are clinically professional. The process may reveal to you that Jackie may see you as ambitious and a threat. Whether that is fact or not is unimportant. If you decide to behave 'as if it is correct' that you are seen as ambitious and a threat, then you can address

---

[1] This process is powerful and called 'second positioning'. For more complete examples and methods, please refer to McLeod (2003).

any such feelings directly. Your approach will change as soon as you have that perception.

Malcolm went through this process in his own Board room. His boss was the outgoing Chairman of the group. He realized that his Chairman needed to be more confident in him and that he should communicate more effectively and more often rather than waiting for the Chairman to call him from his home overseas. He also realized that the Chairman disliked him owning new ideas for business-development. The Chairman wanted to own or be a part of those himself. Malcolm therefore embarked on a process of proactive communication and did more research, providing factual evidence to support arguments. He also talked through ideas at an earlier stage and invited advice. Malcolm also realized that the Chairman liked to remain in control of the big stuff. With one merger idea that Malcolm was very confident about, he decided to introduce it matter-of-factly, saying it was probably not worth looking at and passing the report to the Chairman for his comment and advice. The Chairman was enthusiastic and encouraged Malcolm to press on with the negotiations.

16

Strategic influence

B Y STRATEGIC INFLUENCE I MEAN SOME OF THE GENERAL ways of helping people to think well of you (and of your area) and be more accommodating to your ideas and aims, rather than the individual people skills that we have considered so far. The key to strategic influence must be communication. By that, I do not just mean the broadcasting of information; I mean understanding those who might be influenced, getting the pitch and timing right and if possible seeking feedback to check that the desired result is happening. The following steps may be helpful. Remember that the more senior you are, the more you need to compromise and collaborate to win friendships among the power-players – winning outright becomes less fruitful.

What I need to communicate

This may not be the same as what you want to communicate. If you have a sense of ownership or emotional attachment to the outcome you may need to create calm, objective perception before doing anything – some of that could involve research and discussions with trusted colleagues in order to get the right set up.

What are the implications

Think holistically about the wider implications.

- Who might be for you or against you?

- If you do not know, is it possible to find out?

- Who may be envious of you?

- Who are the other stakeholders and how might they be affected?

- How will they interpret the changes?

- If there is a gap – how will you close that gap?

- Will success or failure place you at risk?

Who is my target audience?

Most of these will be obvious but there may be other stakeholders and power-players who are less obvious. Think about the close relationships your first group of targets – who among them is important to get on-side?

- Is it better to pick off individuals separately or not?

- If a group is involved what will be the preferred method?

- Are there preferences for certain media?

- Would an open forum be favorable if you could get certain people on-side in advance?

- Who would those people be?

Who might I involve before going public?

- Who would really appreciate mentoring you?

- Who would wish to collaborate on all or part of your strategy?

- If such preparation is needed, will this have to start somewhat earlier than the launch of the key messages?

- Are there those who have a pattern of rejection? If they do, could you have a private discussion to offer a contradictory approach and then bring the original one to the table?

- Winning the battle is not always successful if key people feel antagonistic toward you. Is anyone likely to be in that position and can you ameliorate that in your strategy now?

- Are there those who want to control new ideas as their own, and who are influential?

- How can you have an early conversation with them and honor them in the delivery of the ideas, bringing them on-side in that way?

What do they need to know?

What they need to know to have buy-in may be at variance with what you need to communicate, at worst it may be in conflict.

- What are the pros and cons of your policy from their standpoint?

- Can you address the cons (not ignore them) and highlight the pros?

- Is the whole message savory or would it be better to let parts out bit by bit with more welcome news?

- If it is one key set of messages, will this need to be reinforced, how many times, how and when?

Who should broadcast the messages?

- Am I the best person to be the communicator?

- Would the messages be better received from someone else? For example, could the Chairman include a brief synopsis in the annual report to pave the way for the development of the ideas?

- Who else might promote the ideas at any level?

- Who is likely to be most positive and motivated to be involved and support, at any level?

- How can you involve them as thought-leaders?

- What led to any previous failures?

- How have others been successful?

When is it best for them to know?

- What other messages are out there?

- Do I want my message to be dominating or is it best clouded by other issues concurrently.

What will measure success or failure?

- What will happen if you are successful?

- What will happen if you fail?

The strategy for action

Strategy always involves deliberate thought involving thinking-through the consequences and implications of our proposed actions. Many people short-circuit this as it is not obviously productive like many other functions of managing. However, it is exactly this type of enquiry and rethinking that leads to wiser decisions. If we are not to do these ourselves then we need someone else to provide that level of thought in the team.

17

Managing meetings

W HEN WE INITIATE MEETINGS WE NEED TO THINK about the overall purpose. Is the meeting simply to give information and check for understanding that everyone is on the same page? Or is the meeting principally to check progress and exert peer-pressure to perform? Perhaps the main reason is to involve and create new learning and develop new ideas. Whatever the main reason there is little point in having a meeting if people do not understand the desired behaviors and outcomes. A list of subjects (agenda) may just not be sufficient – an agenda quite reasonably looks like a sequential process but does not usually describe the expected behaviors and desired outcomes. And a list is hardly a good start for stimulating creativity!

Agenda frames for behaviors and outcomes

So, firstly, let's reframe our meetings to include not just subjects (for telling, sharing, developing, creating) but also to be

Table 17.1 Preparing for best results	
Agenda frame	*Subject/objective/time*
Show and tell	Tom on merger situation (15 mins)
Performance and priorities (individual and project)	Sales development (45 mins)
Participate and develop	New product (50 mins)
Blue sky	Product adaptation and new markets (50 mins + 50 mins)

specific about the type of activity (behaviors) and outcomes we want. Unless we prepare people to behave and produce, as well as define and understand the subjects, we will not get the most out of any meeting.

In order to achieve that, it helps to set out a number of ways in which people will come together and behave – I call these categories 'agenda frames'.

I suggest that you develop your own categories, but Table 17.1 presents some of my own examples together with example subjects for focus.

For clarity, you could set the scene for each type of agenda frame (AF).

Show and tell

These frames are principally for information to keep one another on the same page. Questions are invited for clarity.

Performance and priorities

These frames are to maintain individual and team perform-ance, identify weaknesses, to be open to the expression of issues and problems, to create support strategies to keep us on track, to define and to redefine priorities in terms of both effort and time span. The facilitator will revolve at each meeting irrespective of the number of frames that are tabled.

Participate and develop (P&D)

P&D frames are tabled to create practical solutions and strat-egies harnessing all the skills and experience in the room. Innovative thought is welcome and we will be quick to develop ideas and slow to judge. The meetings will be facilitated by a Project Head from another Division in return for our facilita-tion of their P&D meetings. This will enable all of us to con-centrate exclusively on the development of ideas and solutions rather than the process.

Blue Sky

These frames are arranged to explore the answers to 'what if' questions and explore innovative solutions, without judg-ment. The Blue Sky meetings are also externally facilitated, and after a refreshment break are followed by P&D frames to hone in on potential or new projects.

Once you set out your own frames, your people know more than the subject heading. They understand and can prepare to behave in a way that will help to achieve the desired outcome. Longer meetings may include several such frames.

Meetings: Factoring for success

Having created new frames for meetings and explained the behaviors expected, you are already ahead of the game. But there are other factors that will improve the benefits obtained from meetings.

Interim activity

Where meetings are regular but have long spaces between them for financial or logistical reasons, it is useful to keep the work of the frames moving ahead by creating interim activity. Traditionally this has been done by having working groups reporting back by certain dates. I prefer focus groups that only survive for one objective and then disappear. You are then creating team-development skills among the participants each time a new group is formed. Having several such focus groups keep the frames in the minds of all participants.

Other interim activity may be the act of asking new questions relating to each frame and diarizing these questions to space them out over the period. These questions will probe for depth of thinking, innovation and consequences and will invite discussion, perhaps via e-mail.

Timings

About 15 years ago I worked in a consultancy business. There was a cultural lack of discipline in meeting-management. Meetings always had a starting time on the hour and often no finishing time. As meetings seldom started on time, people tended to drift in late. Agendas were lists of subjects – none of them giving any indication of the depth of discussion, the expected input from any individual, or the length of any inputs. Typical management meetings would last between an hour and a half and two hours. When the 'any other business' was exhausted and the end of a meeting appeared to have arrived, someone would reopen a previous topic even though that had been discussed in depth and actions agreed. In some meetings, a main Board Director would be invited to open the meeting and then leave. This was uniformly unappreciated and demotivating. Their interest in our Division was simply cost-saving and bottom-line, nothing else.

As the most senior of about eight direct reports to my Divisional Director, I decided to run my meetings differently. I started out by time-tabling meetings at a quarter past or quarter to the hour, giving a budget and target for the duration of the meeting. These were rarely more than 35 or 40 minutes, which was warmly welcomed. People arrived on time (or soon afterwards) and meetings never over-ran the budget. I then started to run meetings at 10 past, 20 past, and so on to get more concentration on starting times – this worked. I do not recall anyone being late again. No one tried to backtrack to earlier subjects. Had they done so, I would have directed them to take it up with one or more of the individuals concerned. When I left the business three years later it gave me pleasure to note that some other senior managers had also started to emulate my meeting policies – the culture had changed.

Involve people

If some people are not contributing, ask yourself why they are there? If they could contribute then you need to have a 1-2-1 to find a way to get the benefits you are seeking. For example, you might seek a tabled report from them or offer training or coaching. Try not to corner shy people in meetings. Invite further inputs and leave a space for the quietest to speak. Rushing from one thing to the next will not help the shyest or most reflective individual to participate.

Notice engagement – vary inputs

Good trainers constantly monitor the 'energy' in the room. If it is low, they may pause and offer a break in proceedings. They may move the discussion forward by asking for a summary from the floor, and then having a break – when people feel that things are coming to a close they can usually regain some energy for a few more minutes.

Observations will tell you what is happening even if you do not have the acute sensing ability of an experienced trainer. Look for side-discussions, doodling, fidgeting, dropping heads, slouching, yawning and the relentless turning of pages.

Day meetings with three breaks, including lunch, could be more productive. Better to quicken the pace from time-to-time and have a minimum of five breaks in the day. Be sure that the lighting is high whenever possible and that the air is fresh and circulating. Discourage snacking and reduce the volume of protein and fat (meat and cheese). Provide quantities of cold drinks and still water, but prohibit alcohol.

Vary the means of delivery (video, slides, white-board and speech) and activity, and pause for breakout discussions in smaller groups. If several people contribute with one medium, invite someone to do it differently and break the monotony.

Spot the thought-leaders

There are always those you can involve for a range of reasons – experts, supporters, the Devil's Advocate, detailed thinkers, etc. In terms of impact, however, there are those who will carry more weight than others, not through assertion or dominance but via *gravitas* or earned respect. Brief these people separately and ask them to be involved with the inputs of your messages or the facilitation of discussion. This will vary the input, change pace and involve other motivators. Ignore status in selecting thought-leaders unless this would be detrimental to the quality of the messages and facilitation – the statement needs to be that you run quality meetings with quality people.

Time-out

There are good reasons to program some time-out into the structure of meetings. We have seen that the outline description for Blue Sky action frames included a break mid-way. The reason for that is to enable reflective processes and creativity from individual dynamics (challenges, comparisons, confidence, etc.). Sometimes we need time-out so that net-working can occur, to enable bonds to be strengthened and alliances to be made. This is especially useful in certain cultures or where delegates are coming from many different locations.

When, in Part One, we considered the effect of thinking instead of really listening, we saw that it caused spaces in which content and meaning are lost. Those spaces are due to a number of internal, mental processes, including rehearsing, interpretation, anticipating, etc. But when people are doing their internal reflection, they are no longer listening! By and large we need people to be engaged in the meeting. But how can we get the benefits of (internal) self-reflection AND have the full engagement of everybody. In truth we cannot, but we can engineer strategies to help!

In meetings where creativity and innovation are required, it is worth building in reflective periods. These quiet periods may only have durations of two or three minutes, and a model for this comes from decades of learning from the training-room where self-reflective pauses are common practice. It would be foolish to ignore their positive impact in the context of meetings. In practice this only requires the making of a silent space:

> *Okay, we have covered a lot of ground in considering the options for moving manufacturing off-shore. Can I have some help putting the flip-charts on the wall and then let's have a five-minute*

period to quietly and individually reflect on what we have so far. There will be time afterwards to discuss any new thoughts.

More good work (and bad) can be done over the coffee machine. You can use that time to try to bring people on-side, to explain aspects privately about your own agenda (that might not be overt) and to hear any reservations and advice that they may offer. Where others can anticipate the direction the meeting is taking, they can discuss and get support from colleagues. If networking at the coffee break ever does work against you, so what? It is better to agree something and all push ahead together than have your policy undermined by stealth later.

Challenging the status quo

I once attended a meeting at the Department of Trade and Industry in London. There were at least 35 people there for several hours. The meeting was so dull that the sensors in the room failed to notice any movement over a duration of 10 minutes and all the lights went off. Someone had to stumble to the door and open it to get the lights back on!

What if we inherit meetings of poor effectiveness? The Chair may have been occupied by the same person for years, too many people may be involved and the output may be dull and not cost-effective. In such cases it is worth considering terminating the meetings and re-creating a new forum for the achievement of set objectives. A new focus or objective that fits another theme in your program for change would appear to be logical, even if unpopular with some.

Rotating facilitators and external facilitation are both worth considering particularly if there is a lack of involvement or people tend to wait for one person to take a lead. One advantage of using externals (even if from another area of the business) is that the participants all have the same function and in that context, similar status. If you have been dominant in meetings and have a protégé that could facilitate, withdraw from one meeting and seek feedback on the result. If you return, do so as a delegate.

Ask the chair of meetings to table a discussion on improving the frequency, duration, location and cost-effectiveness of their meetings.

Honoring

Remember to give credit to those people whose ideas and commitment have moved things forward. If you can do this both privately AND openly you get two separate motivations for the price of one.

18

Developing talent

L EADERS NEVER SURROUND THEMSELVES WITH INCOMPE-
TENT people; they build on solid foundations, not shaky
ground. There are many managers who are simply
afraid to hire talent or develop talent in their people. These
managers often have fragile egos and manipulative abilities.
True leaders are unafraid of competition from their juniors,
and they recognize that the greater the achievement from
their organization, the more respect they create for themselves. They also recognize that their own people skills are a
saleable asset – a talent of their own that makes them more
valuable on the wider work market.

The true leader is also not a fixed set of skills in any context.
They know that they continue to learn and adapt. The manager
who thinks he has no more to learn has a limited shelf-life –
events will overtake him. Leaders research, self-reflect and
change their behaviors. Before looking at specifics let's look
at a method for taking a fresh overview of the character of

your organization[1] with a view to the identification of developmental strategy for people.

Organizational character overview

Imagine for a moment that your whole team is an individual. In other words, what are the average characteristics of the team if represented by one imaginary person. Table 18.1 includes characteristics from a rating of 0 to 10, but you can quite easily create or add your own list of characteristics. In each case, set down your rating for the extent of that characteristic from low (0) through to 10. Leave the third column empty at the moment.

The meaning you give to each characteristic is the only one that matters. Some of your answers will already be qualified. In some contexts playfulness and easy-going might be acceptable, welcome and useful; in others that might not be the case.

In the third column, please now set down the rating that you wish your organization manifested, on average.

When you look at the gaps between scores in columns 2 and 3, you have already established items that will provide immediate ideas for training and development. You will also be able to create a theme for your change strategy which will underpin the desired characteristics, at all levels of organization.

---

[1] Adapted from McLeod (2006).

Table 18.1 List of characteristics

Characteristic	Rating	Desire
Professional	......	......
Energetic	......	......
Sensible	......	......
Successfully innovative	......	......
Open	......	......
Supportive	......	......
Good communicator	......	......
Team-player	......	......
Motivated	......	......
Committed	......	......
Effective	......	......
Expert	......	......
Reasoning	......	......
Measured	......	......
Consequence aware	......	......
Planning for future	......	......
Developer of others	......	......
Considerate	......	......
Builds relationships	......	......
Trustworthy	......	......
Grudge-free zone	......	......
Honest	......	......
Encouraging	......	......
Involving	......	......
Accommodates, compromises and collaborates	......	......
Assertive/direct	......	......
Great listener	......	......
Flexible and enjoys challenge	......	......
Clear vision and goals	......	......
Knowledge of detail	......	......
Adaptive to change	......	......
Organized	......	......
Liked by colleagues	......	......
Liked by stakeholders and customers	......	......
Socializes with colleagues	......	......
Playful	......	......
Easy-going	......	......
Loud	......	......
Aggressive	......	......
Blaming	......	......
Egocentric	......	......
Manipulative	......	......

For example, if the characteristic of 'easy-going' is too high and is creating errors and letting customers down, then it is time to think about replacing (or adding to) existing management systems, documentation and controls at several levels of management. Training would augment those initiatives. The theme for these initiatives might be 'Customer Experience Excellent'. You would probably want to measure that customer experience to monitor their perceptions. Think also about reward and recognition structures internally – what can you offer that would help the objectives?

Part Three

Self-Learning
for Leaders

I N Part One we included a number of typical self-management issues that would provide quick-hits in terms of actions. In Part Two we then looked at aspects of managing that could impact on our leadership of others. In Part Three the objective is to take a deeper and longer pause for thought in order to gain further insights about ourselves and how we think. The aim, then, is to look more deeply into the patterns of thinking that work for us and adjust those in which we can see benefits. All of this demands introspection, learning and personal control over self-development. This is the area from which the next level of performance must arise. We know the objective, we know the job and the people, all that is left to enhance is our thinking – not just in what we do, but in how we impact and create movement in those around us.

Part of this journey, as we will see when we reach Chapter 21 on Emotional Intelligence, also comes from a translation of our self-learning to more exquisite sensing of other people. As these skills develop and grow, so the style and impact of our leadership also develops and grows. The journey tends to be an organic one. Let's see if we can accelerate that journey now.

Modeling leadership

Here is an exercise we do regularly on trainings. It involves thinking about someone who has been an inspiration to you at a personal level. If you are unable to think of someone, then by all means take as your model a significant figure you know something about from the media and whose leadership style is appropriate to best practice in management today. You may have to make some assumptions to fill in the gaps!

Recall someone that has been inspirational to you in terms of their leadership qualities. Ideally, their leadership will have impacted on you and affected you directly. What were the leadership qualities that made them special to you as a leader? Please leave columns A and B blank at the moment.

Leadership qualities of	A	B
....	....	....
....	....	....
....	....	....
....	....	....
....	....	....
....	....	....
....	....	....
....	....	....
....	....	....
....	....	....

Now, please score in column A, your rating for how perfectly you exhibit each quality in your actions at work today (0, low, to 10, high).

When we admire someone we have the chance to hone our own abilities to emulate or 'model' that person. In order to do that, please note in column B those areas where you would like to make a difference in your own style of managing and leading. In each case one or more actions will arise. These might involve trying something out, learning a new skill or getting some development training or coaching. What will you need to learn or practice exactly? What specific things will you do differently, when and with whom?

ACTIONS

19

The Real Thing at work

THE REAL THING COMES DOWN TO UNDERSTANDING that most of us have a wider range of authentic expression than those we bring to work. This chapter aims to bring attention to our authentic competences so that the differences between 'what we do' and 'what we could do' are made overt. That overt understanding will then enable conscious decisions to be taken. Leadership is very much about being more conscious: not only more conscious about the things we seem naturally (and subconsciously) to do well (for there is learning in that) but being more conscious of all our competences to enable us to have more choices for performing at the next level of efficacy.

The Real Thing concerns aspects of self. And in the context of work the effective use of the Real Thing must result in behaviors that are aligned with who you really are. In other words, not an act. Many people do bring an act to work, leaving their real nature at home.

For many people there may be conflict between wanting to do what they feel and think is true to them, and what they think is appropriate at work. Expressing from the Real Thing does raise questions about when it is appropriate (or otherwise) to express (and behave) from a sense of self.

Invariably there are questions about who we are at work compared to who we are in any other context of our lives – and is there a difference? Most managers will say that there is a distinct, indeed a proper, difference, but there are also great leaders who exemplify the contrary argument in all they do – people who, in any context exhibit behaviors that are largely predictable when you understand the driving values and beliefs that form the basis for ALL that they do in the world. Examples probably include the 14th Dalai Lama, Sister Theresa, Nelson Mandela, Martin Luther King Jr, and Mahatma Gandhi. It is trite to argue that any of these people have not led organizations at least as complicated as our own. Each built key relationships, inspired people and create(d) cultural change on a major basis. We have much to learn from them that is applicable to the context of corporate life.

Can we accept also that authenticity is a moving, growing thing? Great leaders distinguish themselves from other leaders by developing into 'what they chose to become'. In other words, they did not see their sense of self as permanent and they did not accept fate; most certainly they had visions of what they could be and moulded and grew to BE what they developed. Do you have a clear vision of the type of leader you will evolve into, or not? Possibly the exercise you completed earlier will have helped define aspects of your leadership and how you will make specific differences. But how will you appear when all those aspects are complete? And if that was now, what are you thinking and doing differently now?

> *Great leaders distinguish themselves from other leaders by developing into 'what they chose to become'.*

When great leaders decide to strive for something extra from themselves, these major shifts in personal vision are driven by one or two simple but inspiring perceptions. Typically these are values or beliefs that become of paramount importance to them. These could be overarching beliefs about their own purpose or their values about justice. These values and beliefs become locked into their sense of identity and dictate how they must 'be' and 'act' in the world.

It may take a painful experience or a revelation to find such a huge association in our values, beliefs, and sense of self and purpose. In some cases it is a dramatic shock or realization from events outside our personal control. Of course we could wait a lifetime for that! If we are to find and define our own vision of leadership then we already know that it will not come while we fire-fight. No, it will arise from openness to learning and periods of self-reflection and growth. Hence the importance of these chapters.

In Chapter 12 in Part Two you were asked to set out your values, beliefs and sense of self that epitomized your sense of leadership and, if relevant, to find a representation for that. This work is that of setting out the direction for the type of leader you want to be. Once you have used that mindset successfully, you will find that you are behaving in an automatic way. This does not run counter to the ethic of authenticity, as we shall see. This is because we are complex, not simple, uniform beings with one attitude for everything.

> *Leaders are never complacent about how much they know; they are mindful of how little they know and strive to narrow the gap.*

Let's explore, firstly, what our own Real Thing is and from there see if there are conscious decisions that can be taken to make a difference, whether toward more 'Real Thing' behaviors or, indeed, less of them. In either case there is potential learning. Leaders are never complacent about how much they know, they are mindful of how little they know and strive to narrow the gap.

Being and doing

Not all my readers will appreciate the notion of a causal link between the sense of self (being) and what we do (behaviors, including actions). Instead, some will say that their actions are more or less sustained by logical thought, learned skills and instinct (due to experience). Whether one believes in the causal link or not, it is helpful to consider our qualities of being (self) as well as our qualities of doing. Introspection into both areas may lead to a number of fresh perceptions, a wider range of choice, and then new actions.

Qualities of being (self)

There is a school of thought that we are not our behaviors. In other words, we are 'I' (identity statement), which is better defined by the qualities of who I am rather than what I do in the world. What is certain is that there are at least two ways of assigning qualities to ourselves: on the basis of both 'being' (identity) and 'doing' (behaviors). Let's start with qualities of being. Please explore the following in order to create a snapshot and leave the right-hand column empty for the moment. For the avoidance of doubt let's define the three areas in Table 19.1:

Table 19.1 Values, beliefs and identities

Values that drive my work
I value:
1 ....
2 ....
3 ....
4 ....

Beliefs that drive my work
I believe that:
1 ....
2 ....
3 ....
4 ....

At work, I have the identity of ...
1 ....
2 ....
3 ....
4 ....

- **Values** – A paramount quality that influences you, e.g. helping people to develop, honesty, friendship, profit, fair terms and conditions.

- **Beliefs** – Things that can be expressed as true even if evidence is weak, e.g. I believe that . . . people want to do the best that they are capable of; holding back information during times of uncertainty is bad for business; one can achieve more if one sets one's goals higher.

- **Identity** – Things that provide a simple description of who you are, e.g. I am a thoughtful manager; expert in business-to-business (B-2-B) relationships; dedicated worker; good developer of people.

Objectively, in the right-hand column, please write down some of the key behaviors that might be expected of someone else who had those qualities of being.

NOTES

- To what extent do you exemplify all these behaviors at work?

- Is there a gap and, if so, where is that gap and what can you do to narrow it?

- How will your actions and behaviors be noticed by others and when?

NOTES

Qualities of doing (actions and successes)

It may be easier to set down some of the qualities that are measurable in the world of your work. These qualities would include the things for which you have a good feeling and where you did well in spite of the odds or your relative lack of ability or experience at the time. Please leave the right-hand column of Table 19.2 blank for the moment. Examples of actions and successes are the sorts of things you might place in a CV as well as things that others might find trivial at your current status but which you felt proud of at the time.

Now, in the right-hand column please note down the key qualities about you – or that you believe about yourself – that made those actions and successes possible.

Table 19.2 Measurable qualities

Actions and successes

1	......
2	......
3	......
4	......
5	......
6	......
7	......
8	......
9	......
10	......

If you now have a list of key qualities for doing things successfully, why not take time to check that you are using these qualities to their maximum benefit when considering the current obstacles and challenges in work today? What could you improve to have a faster or better result?

ACTIONS

Recalibrating authenticity for work

We are not entirely predictable even if, in any one context, people tend to find us more or less consistent. Those who work most closely with you almost certainly hold different ideas about who and what you are than others more remote from you at work. If there is a difference, which group thinks most favorably of you: those close to you, or those more remote?

If those more close to you are likely to think better of you than the others, then that could suggest that your use of the Real Thing in closer relationships is achieving results. The obvious question then becomes: could you behave in that way more widely at work? In practice that would mean extending the behaviors you already use with the closest people and trying them out with others to assess the impact. Factors that might influence the extent to which this extension is advisable were considered in Chapter 9 in Part Two.

If those close to you at work are likely to think of you less favorably than those who are more remote, it is worth considering whether your behaviors with your closest colleagues are appropriate and whether or not they are behaviors that you would consider appropriate among friends, at home or with neighbors. If there is a disparity in your behaviors, then ask yourself why, and whether you have a choice to act differently. Importantly, ask whether, in fact, you actually *can* act differently. If the answer to the last question is no, then I recommend that you hire a good coach as quickly as you can. A small number of people will have dysfunctional relationships in every context of their life, in which case longer term intervention via counseling or psychotherapy might be considered.

But what has all this to do with the Real Thing? Surely we just are, or are not. Actually we are, as they say, different things to different people. Not just because of misconceptions but because, very typically, we are (more or less) subtly different in our behaviors in different contexts. For example, is the level of caring you exhibit uniform for all people at work or do you favor certain people only? Could you do more?

Assuming just for the moment that the statement is true; surely we have choices about how we behave at work that are still 'authentic' or the Real Thing? I believe this to be the case, and to explore it I would like you to consider a process to tease out the range of choices you have – all of them being your Real Thing!

We are very much like stringed instruments. Most people are subconsciously retuning depending upon the context, much like the subtle retuning in an orchestra to work with the acoustic of the chamber. Now perhaps we could also do this retuning, but more consciously and thus create increased choice and dominion over how we behave at work?

Testing the strings

For each of the characteristics in Table 19.3, please think of the extent to which it relates to you in the context of your whole experience of living, not just work. Once again, you might use the scale, 0 (low) through 10 (high) for the level at which you believe it applies to you.

Think of a context for each characteristic where it applies to you least. What score do you give that out of 10? Please place

Table 19.3 Personal characteristics

Characteristic	Lowest	Work value	Highest
Thanking	......	......	......
Appreciating	......	......	......
Honoring	......	......	......
Listening	......	......	......
Supporting	......	......	......
Encouraging	......	......	......
Apologizing	......	......	......
Learning from and accepting failure	......	......	......
Inclusive behaviors involving all	......	......	......
Thoughtful action	......	......	......
Explicit helper	......	......	......
Clear communicator	......	......	......
Clear objectives	......	......	......
Clear boundaries	......	......	......
Attention to details	......	......	......
Decisive in acute situations	......	......	......
Use humor to relieve stress	......	......	......
Flexible approach	......	......	......
Do as you expect others	......	......	......
Measured risk-taker	......	......	......
Can-do attitude	......	......	......
Focus on what you can do, rather than what you cannot	......	......	......
Thoughtful about consequences of action	......	......	......

that score in the 'lowest' column. You might also want to note the context next to each score if there is room.

Then think of the context in which that characteristic applies to you most of all. What score do you give that? Please place that in the right-hand 'highest' column. Having done that, what score (or range) do you give the characteristic as it applies to you in the context of work? Please put that rating in the 'Work value' column.

Humor

All the characteristics above have been mentioned before, except humor. Humor has a place in leadership particularly in relieving stress among colleagues.[1] Stress at the higher levels does get in the way of both logical mental processing and creative thought because of the emotional processing we saw in the Stillness–Activity Dimension. A process for reducing stress in these situations is simple: acknowledge the situation by using 'feeling/sensory' words to express the disappointment/anger/resentment/stress, then invite cerebral activity by posing a question: 'So what can we do now to move forward?'

Often we sit on our humor at work because it may be thought of as unprofessional in acute situations. As we know, humor has been used for millennia to relieve the stress of dire situations, including dying and death. Provided there is a release of stress, then the humor has made a valuable contribution to moving ahead. If you are already funny in your private life then consider being freer with your humor in situations where there is shock or paralysis due to bad news. One short episode of laughter is the fastest way to move from stress to produc-

---

[1] Fun created on a team basis helps to establish team rapport too. As well as humor, activities that involve sharing of personal knowledge help people to trust one another.

tive work. As before, this is followed by a question such as that posed above.

Here are a couple of examples of humor used to destress

Tom: *It's a dog's dinner I'm afraid*
H: *Not so much the dinner but what comes out the other end.*

Tom: *It could not be any worse.*
H: *I guess a fire-bomb might have the edge?*

Tom: *Jenkins is testifying against us.*
H: *Is that worse than when he testified for us?*

Humor is always best used in the moment. If you have found yourself biting your tongue you may wish to think about giving yourself permission to let your natural ability be expressed in stressful situations in future. If you are not sure, then think of those situations when you have bitten your tongue. What do you think would have happened had you made your joke? Would that have generated a better result than what actually transpired?

Tuning for perfection at work

Typically you will find that the range of the Real Thing that you express in the world is wider than the score (or range) that you express at work. It is not surprising if that is so. But the real question is, what choice do you have about WHO you take to work? And what about the other contexts of your life? Could you be more supportive at home, for example?

- Knowing what you do about leaders and leadership, what ability do you have that you have not adequately applied in the field of work?

- In what specific situations might these be useful?

- What behaviors will be different, when and with whom?

ACTIONS

Maintaining progress

In Part Two we looked at typical actions that leaders take and then considered the importance of communication to those around us where our actions and behaviors will be significantly different from before. If we fail in this step, some people will feel neglected, under pressure and so forth. But that is all there is to it. Having carefully considered your actions you know that they are the right ones for you and your people; all that is now needed is to anticipate the possible misunderstandings and communicate to prevent that.

20

Self-awareness for leaders

'Turn weakness into a weapon'

GIANNI RIOTTA

G ENERALLY, THE HIGHER OUR ROLE IN ORGANIZATIONS, the more lonely the job. There is a certain vulnerability that most of us who have held senior posts acknowledge privately. At this level in a career it is very easy for the manager to hold on to the behaviors that have worked in the past. They might imagine that these behaviors may have been part of the reason that they have been hired in the present post. But more senior posts invariably require different behaviors to the ones that brought us to that position. For example, the need to compromise tends to be greater at the top. It may also be necessary to take a more strategic and holistic view of things and have a broader understanding of the consequences of action and change in the longer term.

At the higher levels, the King-makers and power-brokers often become more difficult to spot; there are circles and friendships that are covert because of the political awareness of the players. Managers may think they have arrived in the circle but will often be fooled. There is usually more going on than meets the eye. What have you missed?

A leader needs to be alert to the power of subgroups and know what characteristics will ease his entry into the good books of the most influential circles. It is easy to make a list of stakeholders, but which have the most influence? Some of the most powerful people are not even on the main Board, but work below it.

A significant help in being able to work at this level is to heighten powers of self-awareness. It is the established pattern of self-awakening that distinguishes the leader. Growing self-awareness unpeels the skins of the onion and we see more clearly that those around us are no longer so easy to label. And, as we discover more about ourselves, so we keep gaining deeper realizations about other people, their true character and their motivations. The best option we have in this process is feedback. Firstly, feedback will accelerate our perspective about ourselves, and, secondly, feedback enables us to check that the perceptions we have about others is correct.

Feedback for leaders

How often have you been stung by a judgment made about you by someone close to you? People who are close to us do sometimes misunderstand us or our motives and have judgments about those. If some of the people closest to us do not understand who we really are, what do our coworkers think?

Feedback and self-learning

If you are not already familiar with 360-degree feedback in your organization, or are not currently using it, then the concept of feedback may be prejudiced. 360-degree feedback involves a formal method of seeking feedback on identified personal factors from people above us, below us and our peer group. Formal methods like this are enormously useful, especially if we bite the bullet and include in the list those people we are unsure of or who we feel may be antagonistic toward us. Leaders will unhesitatingly include these categories. They know that here is a golden chance to learn what those people think about them and maybe learn something that is useful in terms of improving their image. Feedback does not accurately make judgments about what you actually do or don't do, rather the judgments are perceptions that people hold about you, right or wrong. If these vary from what you would wish, then there is only one person to fix that perception, and that person is you. This might be a good time to consider the 51 Percent Rule (McLeod, 2006).

The 51 Percent Rule

In any given interaction I am 51 percent responsible for the outcome of that interaction

If we accept 50 percent or less of the responsibility then no action occurs; we have a stalemate. If we take all the responsibility then the chances are that our actions will be neurotic, overbearing, invasive or misinterpreted as aggressive. At 51 percent we must take action, but in a measured and professional way.

What unresolved issues and conflicts do you have in your closet? Is now the time to revisit and see what healing you might stimulate by trying to build rapport and trust?

Remember that it takes two people to party. If you fail to engage after trying a new approach or two, it may be best to withdraw. With luck, the Real Thing will eventually shine through to them. It is also worth enhancing that by engaging with those closest to them. Increasing your personal impact and respect among that group this will tend to filter good vibes from third-parties. This is always a beneficial approach to take.

Whether you have a 360-degree feedback mechanism in place or not, interim feedback can be found all around you. If asking for feedback is a novelty for you, then start simply with those closest to you and work out from there. Questions might go something like this:

You know that paper I put in yesterday – do you think I came across too strident?

I know I let things get off-topic in that meeting but noticed that Diane had not contributed up until then. Do you think I did the right thing?

I've been overdoing it recently due to the year-end rush and may have overlooked needs that you may have had for my time, what do you say?

Did you think I was a good listener when we spoke yesterday?

In each case the question is posed about a single episode in the past. That is deliberate. People are more likely to give you feedback in relation to something you 'did' than to give you feedback about something you are going to do (all the time). They can comment about one specific incident as if it was a one-off, rather than a statement that boxes you.

Any question will have to be in your own words. Remember that if this is new to you, your seeking feedback is also new to those receiving your questions. At first they may be reluctant to tell you anything or be overly polite in their responses. It is therefore useful to have a longer-term strategy for seeking feedback with the same group of people so they get to learn that giving higher quality, direct feedback is in fact okay – you do not bite! In fact, thanking them might be a good thing, particularly if you are able on occasion to say that their feedback has led to a change in what you now do.

Mindset for receiving feedback

A mindset is simply a collection of values, beliefs and sense of self that positively puts you in a psychological position to best deal with a particular circumstance. When it comes to feedback it can be helpful to pause long enough to create a suitable mindset for that situation. It's a little like a boxer raising his hands before a fight and shouting, 'Yes!', or the All Blacks rugby squad performing their Haka.[1] These are some

---

[1] Haka is the generic name for traditional Maori dance.

of the values, beliefs and sense of self that one might find helpful to focus on briefly, before seeking feedback:

- Feedback is only opinion, not truth.

- Feedback gives me options for control of my own development.

- There is value for me in feedback.

- Feedback gives me the chance to correct misinterpretation.

- Feedback gives me the chance to learn to do things better.

- People mean well, however unsubtly they express themselves.

- I learn from feedback.

- I am willing to make changes to what I do.

- I am not defined only by behavior, but also by who I really am.

Feedback to check my interpretation

We considered that feedback is helpful in finding out whether our judgments and intended action are pitched correctly. Self-awareness and experience gradually improve our ability to predict how other people will feel about our judgments and proposed actions. Managers will act on those judgments whether they are right or not. Leaders will, invariably, continue to check that they have things just right. In the process they continue to hone their learning and get better and better at proposing solutions that are accepted, sustainable and supported by others. If urgent decisions are necessary, these will be found to be wise and have foresight that others would miss.

Typical questions might be:

I feel I over-manage you on this project because of its importance, is that right?

I have not touched base with you so often for several reasons; one is that I felt you were increasingly confident of succeeding with the project. That could come across like I have lost interest in you or the project or that I was trying to distance myself from the outcome as we are behind schedule. Confidentially, what is your view on that?

I have been thinking of taking Quality out of your R&D responsibility to allow you to concentrate on the upcoming innovations and relinquish some of the tedium of day-to-day issues. Would that be a welcome or productive change?

You have seemed very tired of late and I have noticed you working later and later. I am assuming you may need an assistant or another Project Head. Is that about right?

As managers and leaders we do make assumptions and judgments and we are, in part, paid to do just that. What distinguishes the leader from the manager is a seemingly natural ability to take the best route. The simple way to learn how to do that is to keep honing one's knowledge – and feedback is the most valuable way to accomplish that. It's the cheapest and most effective education there is!

21

Emotional Intelligence

ENTIRE BOOKS HAVE BEEN WRITTEN ABOUT EMOTIONAL intelligence, and so I do not intend here to give a full account. However, it would be wrong to ignore such an important factor in the context of leadership.

In Part One we introduced the concept of the following equation:

$$EQ + IQ = Success$$

Here EQ means emotional quotient and IQ is intelligence quotient. The equation suggests that those who have higher levels of both intelligences are more likely to be successful. It involves understanding self and others. If you are expert at these concepts, then you are likely to have an easier ride through corporate structures and have more people supporting you and your aims.

IQ is hard to budge although you can become more expert at the tests. In contrast, emotional intelligence is not a fixed quantity. Anyone can improve their ability and most people make big leaps in skill level in their forties. You do not have to wait for life to happen, however. You can accelerate your journey at anytime of your choice. Table 21.1 lists 20 statements that may help you to get some insight to the level of your emotional intelligence now. To what extent is each statement true of you? There are four possible answers: Don't know (DK), low (L), medium (M) and high (H).

The statements in the table are broadly placed in four categories of five each. The first set concentrates on EI as it applies to your self-awareness. The second set of five questions relates to your abilities to self-manage situations with emotionally stimulating content. The third set concerns awareness of the emotional world of people around you, and the fourth relates to your ability to manage in those situations.

If you want, score the results like this:

- For each H add 2 to your tally.

- For each M add 1 to your tally.

- For each L take 1 from your tally.

- For each DK take 4 from your tally.

Table 21.1 Emotional intelligence level

Statement	DK	L	M	H
People never fidget or talk to others when I speak	......	......	......	......
It is very rare that I have enemies	......	......	......	......
I often consider whether my speech is loud or not	......	......	......	......
I am aware of my feelings and can name them	......	......	......	......
My motivation is complex	......	......	......	......
I adjust my speech level deliberately	......	......	......	......
I never lose my professional cool	......	......	......	......
If upset, I continue to listen acutely to what is going on	......	......	......	......
I deliberately change my habits	......	......	......	......
I express my feelings, and do so where it is appropriate	......	......	......	......
I instinctively know if someone is upset	......	......	......	......
People often come to me for help with personal issues	......	......	......	......
I buy presents that I would not necessarily like myself but are appreciated by the recipients	......	......	......	......
I hand-write the greeting on my letters	......	......	......	......
I do more listening than talking	......	......	......	......
I cope well with awkward and embarrassing situations	......	......	......	......
If someone becomes upset I help to deal with that before moving on with any previous discussion	......	......	......	......
I offer support in preference to advice	......	......	......	......
In a meeting I encourage anyone who has not spoken to do so	......	......	......	......
I make adjustments to people's jobs to fit in with their expressed needs and motivations	......	......	......	......

Assessment of the score:

30+   Advanced EI
24–29   Managing level of EI
16–23   Developing level of EI
Less   Low level of EI

Remember that EI does not have to be frozen for all time. There are actions you can take to develop your EI and improve your success.

Working to improve EI

Look at each set of statements to see how well you did. EI tends to develop, firstly, from self-awareness and self-managing (first 10 statements). If you have better scores for the first 10 statements than for the next 10, the chances are that you are already on the right path. However, things are likely to improve more quickly if you already have some medium and high scores in set three and four as well.

If your scores are uniformly poor it is worth concentrating on your self-awareness and self-managing and making development in these areas. You could do a psychology degree to understand others, but that is unlikely to make you a better leader unless you understand more about your self and practice self-management first.

Self-awareness

Self-awareness is generated by posing questions, listening to feedback and being open to self-challenge.

The questions can be generated by self and by others (feedback) and the feedback can be informal (as described above) or by formal methods including 360-degree feedback. All feedback has to be encouraged as self-challenging will miss many of the most persistent patterns of behavior. The automatic nature of patterns tends to make them invisible to the person who exhibits them. Coaching is a perfect set-up for improving self-awareness since coaching involves the provision of accurate and specific feedback that is entirely honest and given in a supportive environment.

The questions need to target all the following and more.

Be challenging about:

• What you believe.

• Why you do what you do.

• The patterns you have and how useful those patterns are right now.

• Whether you have other choices available to you in belief, behavior and action.

• Whether you are able to exercise all those choices by will, even if you are resistant to doing so.

Roger Sperry Brain Theory

Roger Sperry shared a 1981 Nobel Prize for his work on the dualistic nature of the brain. The left brain was determined as principally logical and the right as more artistic, creative and conceptual. In the West, there is a predominance of left-brain activity but this means that people miss out on much of the benefit that right-brain thinking would give them. On balance, one would expect that using both sides would be better than being mainly restricted to just one!

If you are highly logical, think about challenging your right-brain activity. You can do this by reading novels and poetry, by creative writing, drawing and exposure to art and artistic creation generally. Playing any instrument, particularly if you learn to play by ear, also stimulates the right brain. Not only do these activities create Stretch Zones for the mind, but they also open up new perceptions and spontaneous, creative thought. That is because right-brain processes tend to be more holistic than detailed and because they stimulate the discovery of tenuous links that can be missed by logical processing.

If you are very right brain but not very logical and ordered, then it would be good to find a hobby that involves detail like genealogy, historical research or a study of a genre of writing or art that interests you. All these activities would help.

When we stimulate underused parts of the brain, we tend to have creative moments, memorable dreams and breakthroughs of perception.

ACTIONS

Self-management

Feedback is again the most effective method of challenging our perceptions since, with a high IQ, we can quite easily fool ourselves.

I can think of a few individuals who are very knowledgeable about human development but do not recognize deeply dysfunctional patterns of their own. They also reject feedback by making counter-arguments and reinterpretation. They are highly left-brain thinkers. They are fixed in their perception of themselves and slow to develop. Interestingly, they are manipulative. They think they have 'arrived' in terms of personal development, and this arrogance explains their very gradual evolution.

Coaching is a transforming intervention to experience. To be coached it is important that you are willing and that you have a managing level of emotional energy to sustain the changes. Also, ask yourself on a regular basis, 'as a result of introspection, what beliefs, values and behaviors have I changed this month?'

Revisiting the busy head syndrome

Before continuing to investigate the EI approach to awareness of others, it is worth revisiting the busy head syndrome. Many very capable people have heads constantly filled with dialogue and processing. In Part Two we looked at the impact that failure to listen can have on the people we relate to in work, but here it is worth going deeper into the options for change for those readers who want a quieter, more reflective mindset, whatever their current level of mental processing.

We already considered new approaches to the working day to avoid the potential for lock-in syndrome but there are other things we can do to retrain ourselves to have quieter heads. As we saw with the management of patterns, it is important to know where the triggers are for the syndrome and be able to recognize the earliest possible effect. From there, it can be simply a case of interrupting oneself with a statement or question that recognizes choice:

- *I do not need this, what would be more beneficial to me now?*

- *Who or what needs my attention now?*

- *Be your own Devil's Advocate – what is the argument for the opposite of what I have been thinking up to now?*

- *What would a fly on the wall make of what is happening now?*

- *If someone had great advice for me now, what would it be?*

- *Step back from this.*

For further information about pattern breaking and the use of anchoring positive psychological states (state management), see McLeod (2003).

Awareness of others

Awareness of others is generally driven by the increasing awareness and management of ourselves in terms of our emotional world. This normally introduces a higher level of interest in other people in all but the most insular and dysfunctional. There are those who clinically develop knowledge about how people work and what makes them tick. However, clinical knowledge without excellence in the self-awareness and self-managing aspects is likely to make them insensitive, judgmental and poor at building high levels of working trust and rapport. Knowledge is not the same as understanding. Unfortunately I know no short-cut to understanding!

However, as we gain insights, right or wrong, we learn more quickly if we check the ultimate source of information – the object of our insights. This relates again to the use of seeking feedback to see whether your insight is on track or not. If you already have some interest and insight, then questions will help you to improve the quality and precision of your observations.

Tom, I think I may have missed something yesterday when you were talking about beach holidays. Were you looking for some time off?

Tom, it's almost a year since your son died so tragically – did you want to take time off or want to work through that anniversary?

Tom, I think I may have been overbearing with Daphne yesterday. I'm not sure if she is upset with me or not. What do you think I could have done better exactly?

Tom, I have been running these eight o'clock breakfast meetings for over a year, do you think that we should continue to start them before normal work-time?

All these assume a level of insight or observation skills. You can see that if the skills were very low it might be difficult to know where to start in order to improve. Seeking feedback will provide learning that is helpful to your own self-awareness and to the awareness of others. As you become more relaxed about feedback, so the process quickens – people will give you better-quality information.

Managing others

In the context of EI, this evolves naturally from awareness of emotional factors in other people and taking action to honor those factors and move forward. When people are upset, their issue will cause an inner experience that reduces their ability to think logically and excellently about any particular issue you may both be considering. For that reason, the good manager will pause the conversation and attend immediately to the emotional issues. Only when the feelings have been healed can that individual contribute fully to the business in hand.

Managing these situations has a loop which further stretches our own emotional awareness and ability to self-manage. In situations where someone is genuinely affected, perhaps even crying, your own abilities are tested. In time we learn to manage our own (emotional) state and to be able to hold the space for others; we breathe easily and provide time for them to express anything they need. We also learn to give quiet attention and to hold back from judgment.

For many managers the whole business of developing EI can appear to be like lighting a firework! In practice we are typically tested in stages and the extremes of situation do not reach us until we are ready to handle them. I write this because there does seem to be an innate level of EI in all of us, most of the time. In other words, at a feeling level, however basic, we know when and with whom it is safe to confide. It's the same for most other people too – they are unlikely to explode near you until you are ready!

Epilogue

W E KNOW THAT LEADERSHIP IS NOT JUST WHAT ONE does; it is an attitude of mind that manifests in authentic behaviors, including actions. For that reason alone, leadership is a journey of self-development and not simply a methodology of learning. The leader is invariably changing and developing and courageous in being seen as someone that is developing as a human being and leader, not just having a fixed managing persona. The quickest way forward, therefore, is to keep applying what works for you and to keep seeking feedback from others. The moment we become detached, isolated or arrogant, we have ceased to hone and develop our leadership and begin to decline. Real leaders are self-refreshing themselves as a philosophy of being. They are also what they sought to become – not in position or influence, but in their mindsets, what they believe, what they value and their authenticity of expressing themselves in all they do, in all contexts. It is a journey without an end. May your journey continue to be fruitful, uncomfortable and treasured!

References

Carnegie, D. (1994) *How to Win Friends and Influence People.* Hutchison (Random House), London.

Covey, S. (1990) *The 7 Habits of Highly Effective People.* Simon & Schuster, New York and London.

Gardner, H. (1983) *Frames of Mind: The Theory of Multiple Intelligences.* Basic Books, New York.

Lawley, J. & Tompkins, P. (2000) *Metaphors in Mind.* Developing Company Press, London.

Maslow, A. (1943) A Theory of Human Motivation, *Psychological Review*, **50**, 370–396.

McLeod, A. (2003) *Performance Coaching: The Handbook for Managers, HR Professionals and Coaches.* Crown House Publishing, Carmarthen and New York.

McLeod, A. (2004) Performance Coaching and Mentoring in Organisations, *Resource*, **1** (1), 28–31.

McLeod, A. (2006) *Me, Myself, My Team: How to be an Effective Team Player Using NLP.* (2nd edition). Crown House Publishing, Carmarthen and New York.

Rose Charvet, S. (1997) *Words That Change Minds.* (2nd edition). Kendall-Hunt Publishing, Dubuque, IA.

Senge, P., Scharmer, O., Jaworski, J. & Flowers, B. (2004) *Presence: Human Purpose and the Field of the Future.* The Society for Organizational Learning Inc., Cambridge, MA.

Thomas, K. & Kilmann, R. (1974) *Conflict Mode Instrument.* Xicom, New York.

Index

Index compiled by Terry Halliday